The Flexifoil book of
Power Kiting

Navigator Guides Ltd
The Old Post Office, Swanton Novers
Melton Constable, Norfolk NR24 2AJ
info@navigatorguides.com
www.navigatorguides.com

Acknowledgements

Navigator Guides would like to thank all those at Flexifoil International for the enormous contribution they have made to the publishing of this book, but a special mention to Jeremy Pilkington for the introduction to Jeremy Boyce, an inspired choice of writer, to Alan Pritchard for the design, Jane Rankin for all her help and to Andrew Jones and Mike Shaw for their technical advice and input. Likewise, Paul Thody from Air Born Kites, Matt Taggart from Ozone Kites and J from ATB Mag. for special technical advice. To all you mad people out there who keep making it all happen. And finally to Jeremy Boyce for all his hard work and constant enthusiasm for the project.

Design concept.Alan Pritchard
www.baldheadmedia.com

Illustrations by Liz Johnson
Contributors: Andrew Jones and Mike Shaw
Photographers: Alan Pritchard, Andrew Jones, Carol Kohen, Christian Black, Dan Eaton, Jono Knight, John Carter, Ray Merry, Ronny Kiaulehn and Jane Rankin
Proofreading: Susannah Wight
Colour reproduction: PDQ Digital Media Solutions Ltd
Printed in Italy by Printer Trento srl

The Flexifoil book of
Power Kiting

Jeremy Boyce

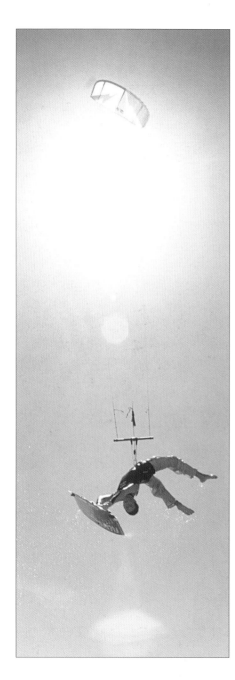

Contents

Foreword

AFTER TRYING MOST extreme sports at one time or another during my life, and loving each one for whatever buzz they had to offer, I had no idea that powerkiting would end up being my big passion. Power kites really have got something for everyone whatever your level.

Flexifoil is all about the power kite and they've been involved in inventing, developing and promoting power kites for nearly 30 years. I first got involved with Flexi in 1994, and I've flown and tested every Flexifoil kite to their absolute limits. Flexi believed in me and my ability with their power kites. With Flexifoil's support I went on to become British, European and World Champion on a kite buggy.

In 1997 Flexifoil made a now infamous trip to Senegal, West Africa, to make a promo movie involving all aspects of the sport, to show the world what can be achieved with loads of powerkite kit and 10 crazy guys imaginations. The resulting 'PowerTrip' video showed people what was really possible with a kite power at that time. This was just the beginning but we soon showed all kinds of madness we could use kites for: mountainboards, buggies, rollerblades, body dragging, man lifting, water skiing and, ultimately, for kiteboarding.

This is where my life started to take a new direction: onto (mostly into at the beginning) the water.

At this stage the Blade kite was in its infancy, a conventional ram air traction kite being designed primarily for land-based buggying and the high end of power kiting. Its elliptical shape, advanced profile and well balanced bridle made the Blade great for the new sport of kiteboarding as well as one of the best performing and best loved power kites ever produced. The Blade is now better than ever, in its third generation and still one of the best high end ram air kites around. It's been joined by the Bullet, a super-stable, entry level buggy kite that delivers great power too.

After competing internationally with the Blade I and II since 1999, the Flexi rider and design teams realised that the next kite would have to be fully water re-launchable. The new Storm II has established the company as a serious competitor in the potentially huge inflatable kite market and our rider team as one of the best in the business.

When you think about the potential crossovers from so many other sports like surfing, windsurfing, sailing, snowboarding, skiing, water skiing, paragliding, skateboarding, mountain boarding etc. the future for the power kite looks huge. And when you've believed in this sport for as long as I have, its fantastic to see the whole thing booming. I'm really excited to see what the future has to hold.

Jason Furness, Flexifoil sponsored rider
August 2003

◄ *Jason in action*

History

Introduction

IT'S BEEN NEARLY 30 years since the development of the first steerable stunt kites, and over 15 since the appearance of the first commercially available kite buggy heralded the kite traction revolution that has brought power kiting to where it is today, standing on the verge of a breakthrough into the big time courtesy of the now massively popular buggy and the new, sexy, kite god, kiteboarding. One company has proudly stood astride all these milestone events and years with a name, reputation and commercial success built, in the beginning, on one highly original product, probably the most ubiquitous kite product and name in the world today: Flexifoil. During all that time they've been guilty of providing the kite industry with more entertainment and adrenaline moments, more craziness and controversy, than any other kite company anywhere in the world. This is the epic tale of the rise and rise of Britain's finest and the world's best-known kite traction manufacturer, Flexifoil International.

The history of Flexifoil is the kind of story that, if you wrote it as fiction, nobody would believe it could really happen, filled, as it is, with luck, pluck, skill, chance, fate, accident, heroic endeavour, considerable peril, immense challenge and fantastic adventures. Ultimately the most incredible thing is that it's taken so long for their outstanding invention to grab the popularity it has,

◀ *The Euro stack of 6' Flexifoils*

triggering so many spin-off activities (from simply flying the kites) along the way. Like any famous invention its arguable that someone else would have thought of it if Flexifoil hadn't but, the point is, they did. And its certainly true that there are now dozens of designers and manufacturers of highly competitive traction kites fuelling a rapidly growing industry, such is the current worldwide interest in kite powered possibilities perhaps they all owe their start in life to Flexifoil. You could say that Flexifoil have made possible the whole traction scene as we know it today.

How it all began

To get the full history you have to make your way back through the mists of time to the mid 70s, back to a time when there were no stunt kites to be bought of any description. Then, madcap British inventor Peter Powell came up with his eponymous, diamond-shaped, long-tailed stunter.

Around the same time, somewhere near Newcastle-upon-Tyne, two design students – Andrew Jones and Ray Merry – were experimenting with wind sculptures and facial hair. They had built a series of sky tubes of increasingly scary dimensions (although they lacked a serious lifting device for them, resorting to long poles and buildings to get them off the ground) before embarking on their ultimate project, an inflatable air-foil wing sculpture that could be tethered as a piece of temporary, movable, public art. They even mocked up photographs of a field and, typically ambitiously, of the Grand Canyon, with their creation superimposed, showing

clearly, even at this early stage, the instantly recognisable profile of the Flexifoil power kite wing. Although they started experimenting with wind as early as 1972, it wasn't until the late 70s, after a lengthy series of wind tunnel tests, that the first "Flexifoils" appeared, made from polythene with an externally fitted cane leading edge rod, but in essence the same kite that is still manufactured today as the top selling 6' Stacker.

The beginnings of success

The two students quickly realised they were on to something as the kites were selling as fast as they could make them, which wasn't actually all that quickly since they were still working from home and doing everything themselves. They switched to wooden ramin dowel leading edges and then to ripstop nylon sailcloth before finally hitting on the fibreglass front spar still used to this day. The kite's performance improved and a small workshop opened with British kite legend Jilly Pelham working on the pre-production prototypes and as one of the very early seamstresses, as Jones is happy to admit, 'setting the standards of Flexifoil's manufacture even in those early days'.

Unable to keep up with rapidly increasing demand Jones and Merry licensed the manufacture and distribution of their product to a new company owned by Eric Gibson who actually came up with the name 'Flexifoil'. All appeared to be going well for 'The Flexifoil Kite Company' until for no apparent reason Gibson disappeared leaving a large prepaid order for kites from a Dutch company and no kites to supply.

The Dutch connection

Desperate for Flexifoils the Dutch customer decided to take on the manufacturing project themselves. Merry and Jones were forced to sell the company, though happily never the ownership of their invention, henceforth earning a royalty on sales from the re-founded Flexifoil company. 'Flexifoil International', as it would be known, was now owned by a Dutch company with business interests in both Britain and Holland.

From the low they found themselves in at the beginning of the 80s, Jones and Merry were about to enjoy a period of sustained, if at first slow, progress and the final realisation of their original vision. Under its new owners, the van Dort brothers, Flexifoil International was moved briefly to Holland and it was during this period that Joost Meojerink joined the company in the general manager cum trouble-shooter role he holds to this day. Around this time the bigger sized Flexifoils began to appear, first the Super 10 then the monster Hyper 12. These focused the impressive pull into single kites rather than the large stacks (trains of kites linked together and flown on one set of control lines) of the original 6' kites.

Also, their invention was beginning to be attached to various objects with the idea of generating other forms of lift or some kind of traction. They had already toyed around with some crude home-made buggies and soon to come would be the kite-powered (a heaving stack of Super 10s) sailing boat,

Jacob's Ladder. Both gave a significant pointer towards future success. Much, much stranger was the model aeroplane toy with a Flexifoil wing that hit the early 80s modeller market as the unfortunately named 'WindBag' For some unaccountable reason this catchy name failed to capture the public imagination and it would be fully ten years before scooting along on a kart, carving up the surf and moonwalking huge kite jumps down the beach would bring those early lift and traction efforts to a workable and, crucially, saleable conclusion.

In the mid 80s Ray Merry left Europe for America to set up Cobra Kites with whom Flexifoil has since maintained a design and distribution exchange relationship. Indeed Cobra has been responsible for subsequent major mutual commercial successes including the 'Scorpion' delta wing sport kite and

▶ *Top: Ray Merry and Andrew Jones*
▶ *Bottom: Sky tubes: Early experiments*

more recently the big selling 'SkyTiger' traction foils. At the beginning of 2003 Flexifoil turned this page of their history, ending production of Cobra designs and finding a new American distribution partner better suited to their updated needs from a vastly changed traction kite market. While the Merry – Jones link is now officially a thing of the past, Flexifoil remains very much about the present and future.

For reasons personal to the van Dorts, Flexifoil International moved back to Britain Newmarket, Cambridgeshire – in 1989. As the kite industry generally 'took off' in the economic boom of the mid and late 80s, Flexifoil soon established itself as the major player in the UK and European market, their kites top of the shopping list for the numerous new kite shops that were opening up at that time.

The rest, as they say, is history. As the 80s turned into the 90s Flexifoil have shown themselves always to be among the market leaders in terms of product development and promotion, with one eye constantly cast on the need for progress and innovation, the other on protecting what they've already got. There are always new products and refinements coming through which reflect or more often anticipate shifts in the market; everything is carefully protected by series patents, continuously updated to reflect the company's meticulous approach to design innovation and improvements. Only recently have they allowed some supplementary production to start up away

▶ *Right: Stack of Stacker 6s*
▶ *Far righ: An awesome stack of Hyper 12s*

from their present factory unit in Soham, to which they moved in the early 90s. Moving production from under their watchful gaze to a remote location abroad has been done simply to cope with the extraordinary demand there is for their kites. Nowhere is this more true than with the kiteboard market where almost all the 'brand' wings you'll find on the market today are made in the far east.

Flexifoil has, for a long time, led the kite industry in professionally promoting and advertising its products, keenly aware that as far as persuading punters to part with their money is concerned, seeing is believing.

Which explains high profile stunts such as the 1999 kiteboard channel crossing and the legendary Le Touquet 208 stack, a single stack of 208 6' Flexifoil Stackers anchored to two giant bulldozers on a Normandy beach in 1994. They've also, over the years, published a series of high-quality colour glossy catalogues and promo materials marking the brand as part of the extreme sports package that is so popular nowadays; club style graphics and radical videos are taking the company image exactly where their future lies.

For many years Flexifoil's 'Battlebus' trade show stand, complete with video wall, demo

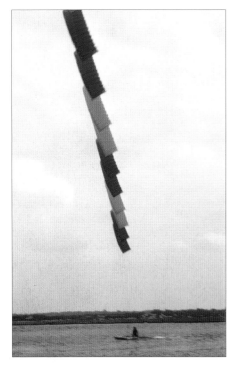

products and knowledgeable enthusiastic staff, probably did more to sell kites of all descriptions than any other single thing in the UK kite industry ever. Except perhaps for their ground-breaking (for the kite business) series of promo videos, each progressively more radical and streetwise. That process has brought us to the present day Flexifoil videos with all the latest kiteboard, buggy, land-board and jumping, radical footage, complete with street music soundtrack, helping them sit easily alongside the snowboard, windsurf,

▲ *Yachtsman Ian Day on Jacobs Ladder powered by Flexifoils*

▲ *Above right: The windbag*

paragliding, skateboard and videos down at your local extreme or street sports shop. The Battlebus too is consigned to history now but Flexifoil's outstanding in-store product displays can now be found in many of the hundreds of Blacks (Camping), Free Spirit, Air and Milletts shops as well as other radical sports shops all over the UK. That's Flexifoil, though, pushing the limits of product performance in the field and commercially.

The future is bright

Having led the kite market as fast and far as it can go, the new Flexifoil objective has been to take their products out to the markets that seem most compatible with them.

That's one reason why there's such a big effort going into the kiteboard side, with instructors and windsurf shop owners (who are stocking kites and other kiteboarding equipment in a big way as the sport really takes off) having been seriously inducted into the dos and don'ts of power kiting before getting into the interesting stuff out on the water. That's also why they employed Jason Furness, ex-kite buggy world champion, one of Britain's leading and pioneering kiteboarders (not to mention 6th placed at the 1999 World Championships in Hawaii), as their hard-working demonstrator, instructor and stunt-puller-in-chief as far as promoting that side of their business is concerned. And that's also why Flexifoil were happy to organise their 'controversial' 1999 cross Channel stunt, irritating French kiteboarders and immigration officials but nevertheless gaining far more in their traditional target areas of exposure and notoriety. As a sign of how times have moved on, Furness has now been joined on the Flexifoil rider – promoter roster by a superb international kiteboard rider team that includes the talented teenage freestyle star Aaron Hadlow, reformed windsurfer and big wave hunter Chris Calthrop, the explosive Danny Seales and female power surfer Andreya Wharry, all Brits of course, as well as star American wave rider Peter Trow and rising German star Petra Goesch.

Sitting quietly at his computer at Flexi's industrial unit headquarters taking it all in you'll normally find the same Andrew Jones (less hair, better trousers), still their designer (their recent and highly successful Blade traction foil is one of his) and tinkerer-in-chief, as well as co-ordinating workshop production, sourcing and acquiring materials when and where they're needed. Until very recently, at the next desk, when he wasn't off somewhere filming himself or someone else doing something unspeakable with a kite, was the other half of the Flexi design team, the unmistakably dreadlocked Andy Preston: master pilot in all disciplines, mastermind behind the Stranger, Psycho, Matrix and Erazor sport kites as well as significant contributor to the design of the Blade and Nexus traction wings. Preston was like a kid in a toy

shop, running loose in the Flexi workshops, design room and factory, constantly tweaking and resewing kites, testing, tweaking again, testing again and so on and so on. Between them Jones, never happier than when he's out test flying, and Preston gave Flexifoil their edge in product development.

Preston has since left to start his own business in kiteboarding but the all-important edge has been more than retained by the recent shackling of designer Henry Rebbeck to the Soham drawing boards. Rebbeck came from nearby Cambridge University to bring some expert technical know-how to the latest challenge facing Flexifoil, developing and manufacturing the fully relaunchable water kite the market dictated they must have. His work on the Storm and Storm II has helped Flexifoil respond to the big league challenge and potential of the incredibly fast developing kiteboard market. He's now been joined by his brother, Luke, an aeronautical engineer from Imperial College, London, bringing yet more high-level technical ability to the

▸ *World record stack of 208 Flexifoils in 1993*

design team. He has worked extensively on the Blade III as well as on the Storm II. Otherwise, Flexifoil have concentrated on their strength in kites and commissioned designs or accepted project submissions for other elements of their product range: extreme driver Rob Hills has worked on the Flexifoil buggy, the landboard project came from designers G2A and their kite control bars are designed by Pete Spence a valuable member of the design team also responsible for the control bar on the Storm II and the Bullet, Blade bar safety system.

The addition a couple of years ago of Sales and Marketing Manager Jeremy Pilkington to the company's ranks has given them a commercial cutting edge and paid huge commercial dividends.

Already the new water wing, the Storm, has established Flexifoil in the inflatable and tube kite market (helping riders Danny Seales and Andreya Wharry to 3rd and 2nd place respectively at the 2002 European Kiteboard Championships), a position which Aaron Hadlow and the Storm II have already advanced some way further. Flexifoil is optimistic about its future. The development of a new ram air traction wing, the Bullet, and of a brand new range of kite landboards in 2003 shows their continued willingness to enter new territory in the search for ever more diverse traction thrills. The stakes are high but the possibilities are limitless. Wherever they end up, as Jones himself says "Its just great to use the wind to go somewhere".

▸ *Top: Channel crossing 1999*
▸ *Bottom: The Flexifoil team 2003*

Basics

"I've jumped out of planes and everything but for me the buzz you can get from power kites stands on its own – something you have to have a lot of respect for, but with big rewards for sure."

Jason Furness, Flexifoil-sponsored kiteboarder and demonstrator, ex World Champion kite buggier, traction junkie

One line good, more lines better

THERE ALMOST COULDN'T be anything much more simple than flying a two or four-line stunt or power kite. Think bike riding without the complication of pedalling to keep moving. To control the kite (bike) you move the handles or control bar push-me-pull-you style, pull right to turn right, pull left to turn left, hands parallel to go straight. All good kites (or 'wings' as the kiteboarders call them) come with instructions but there are all kinds of dos and don'ts that you pick up with experience that help build your comprehension of how the wind and the kites work together to deliver the result you're looking for, – endless hours of fun and amusement. It may be simply for pleasure or it might all come together one day to save your own or someone else's life. No amount of instruction books and videos can make you into the perfect pilot because, ultimately, there's no substitute for getting out there and flying.

Once you get a two-string power kite flying you can completely control it and manoeuvre it exactly where you want it to go. The kite will want to move forwards almost all the time and it's up to your piloting skill to keep it moving around without crashing into the ground or into any other kites, also to make sure that the flying lines

◀ Simple kite maintenance
▶ Traction kite guru Andy Preston flying a Stacker

never get so twisted by repeated turns in one direction that you lose all response from the kite. It might sound complicated but it actually requires less mental and physical agility than many everyday activities such as using a mobile phone, driving a car or, as most people seem to prefer, both at the same time.

And it doesn't stop there as there is also a whole generation of manoeuvrable, traction kites out there with not just two but four control lines that are even more technically sophisticated, more controllable, that can, in the right circumstances, be manoeuvred even more precisely to deliver even more consistent power and efficiency, yes, even programme your video for you... They have helped take power kiting to where it is today, a sport with many layers of sophistication and enjoyment and general ease of use that explains much of the enormous present day popularity for power and traction kiting as an extreme sport and leisure pursuit. In short, a sport on the verge of greatness.

What is power kiting all about? What's the crack?

"I first got hooked on the idea in about 1988, I saw this guy flying a stack of Flexis. He lost all control, came flying past me and my brother at about mach 10 upside down, shot through the middle of a football game using the players as brakes 'til his kites hit the ground. I was on the floor crying with laughter, at the same time thinking 'I've gotta try that'."

Jason Furness, Flexifoil team kiteboarder and tester

Clearly we would in no way condone anyone flying out of control and dangerously close to other people as this reckless pilot appears to have done. Nevertheless, the short answer to the question 'What is power kiting all about?' is the flying of large single or stacked (several kites linked together) manoeuvrable kites in such a way as to achieve traction, that is, be dragged around, and often above, your chosen flying site by whatever means possible. This can include: skidding or skudding (being dragged along on your feet or back), jumping or getting airs, body surfing, buggying or karting, mountainboarding, rollerblading, boating, water skiing, skiing, snowboarding and, in many ways now power kiting's 'market leader', kiteboarding or kitesurfing.

The longer and somewhat more considered version of this is that power kiting is all

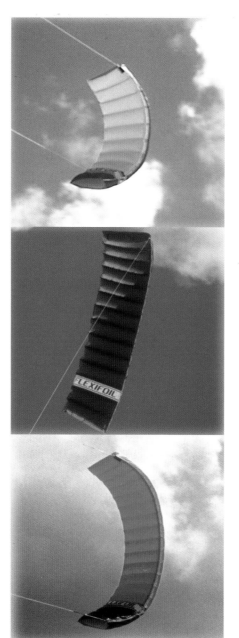

◄ *From top: Stacker 6, Proteam 8 and Super 10*
▶ *Flexifoil's Aaron Hadlow in action*

all about learning how to use the elements, in this instance the wind and your physical location, in a safe and controlled manner so as to deliver the maximum enjoyment with the minimum risk. Power kiting qualifies for listing as an extreme sport and that means extreme injuries, even death, can occur (and indeed have occurred) if the proper respect and attention are not paid to what you are doing. That starts with yourself and applies equally to your equipment and the weather conditions on the day. It means being certain that you know what you're doing and that you understand your limits and your equipment's limits and potential. Whatever level you're doing this at, either for pure recreational pleasure now and then or because you want to be a star rider on the kiteboarding pro tours, you must understand properly how your kite works before you start taking risks. Of course it's accepted that the attraction of extreme sports is the risk and consequent adrenaline rush that comes with it. The trick is making the risk whether you succeed or not rather than whether you end up in hospital or not.

Successful power kiting means working out where your limits are and pushing them gradually further and further until you reach your desired level of skill and 'buzz' that, for many, it's all about. Like many power kiters, you may find that, once hooked, you can never get enough, always looking for more power and more danger (going faster, jumping higher, and so on). That buzz comes at a

price, though, one you should start paying straight away by reading the following safety advice rather than paying later in hospital.

Safety

Walk, don't run

It's vitally important so it's worth repeating until it becomes a mantra:

Safety is the responsibility of the flyer!
Safety is the responsibility of the flyer!

Just like most other extreme sports, especially if you're going to be taking it up in the air or onto water — the sea, you need to totally familiarise yourself with your equipment at the outset. Learn how to properly control a kitewing of manageable size before you start risking life and limb on any of the large number of serious traction and sport wings on the market today. Once you've mastered the basics you'll be ready to get going with some of the big, adrenaline-inducing wings with which Flexifoil is synonymous. All the same, be ready to be shocked and surprised by just how much 'grunt' these wings can generate and never underestimate what can happen when you start playing around with the elements, such as wind and or water, or both. What you take the time to learn today might well save a life tomorrow, your own or that of a colleague.

It's worth remembering that a kite is a sail, just like on a boat, and that the bigger the kite the greater the power it can generate.

The risk of personal injury is ever present and, as an opening piece of advice, let's say that if you are one of those people who falls hard and breaks easily then maybe power kiting isn't for you. If, on the other hand, you know how to fall without hurting yourself and you bounce rather than break then read on. You will need a reasonable level of fitness if you want to really get to grips with the big power generators. If you don't already have good fitness you will need to build that up by flying smaller kites to begin with before moving onwards and upwards, literally and metaphorically. Torn muscles and tendons can easily happen, injuries that take time to mend and will keep you off the flying field for lengthy periods. Broken wrists, ankles and collar bones can too easily result from heavy landings on hard surfaces. In any event you will find, after your first couple of sessions, that power kiting works on different muscles and in a different way than you are used to. Expect to feel some aches and pains in unusual places as your body adjusts.

With the speed of technical innovation there has been in power kiting recently, there are now lots of pieces of equipment and safety aids available to the modern power kiter, in many cases tagged onto the kites (this is specially so in kiteboarding). Harnesses are common in kiteboarding and buggying otherwise you couldn't cope with the huge pull of the kites for any length of time. Never, however, under any circumstances permanently attach yourself to the kite(s). No matter how good and experienced a kite flier you are the unexpected can always happen and you may need to separate yourself from the kite quickly. Quick releases, de-power systems, flotation jackets, crash helmets, knee and elbow pads, goggles etc. etc. are all part of the power kiter's essential equipment nowadays. But never forget that the first level of safety is the flier him or herself. Honesty and awareness about your own skill level and experience, understanding your equipment and the conditions on the day, can all save you an immense amount of trouble or injury.

Whatever equipment you've got, you'll need to check it over frequently for wear and tear. Equipment failure at an inopportune moment, especially out on the water up in the air, or both, could have serious consequences. Take or send equipment back to your dealer or the manufacturer. Many kites and other pieces of equipment are guaranteed against faulty manufacture or unexplained failure. That's not an invitation to trash your kite to bits and expect it to be repaired or replaced free of charge. There are clauses about 'normal wear and tear' in all guarantees and retailers and manufacturers are eagle-eyed. They can spot mistreatment a mile off. Look after your equipment and it will look after you. Get repairs done without delay. In any event, money spent on a repair could be a life saver and there's no price on that.

◀ *High-speed buggy wipeout*

Safety is more than just a personal issue. A little carelessness or over enthusiasm can mean crashing your kite into or onto spectators and passers by. Whilst many power kites are, in principle, soft (no rigid frame parts) they can, as we have said, generate enormous power and cause serious injury. But it's not just the kite itself that can be dangerous. Between you and the kite can be anything up to 45 metres (150 feet) of flying lines which will be moving through the air under extreme tension. The flying lines are thin, made from high-quality, lightweight materials to reduce drag and make the kites more efficient. This is a potentially fatal combination as, when flying a reasonable-sized power kite, the effect of the pull and tension gives the lines a cutting capability similar to cheese wire. There are countless stories of careless power kiters losing fingertips or severing ears with their flying lines. Always disable your kite and flying lines on the ground when you are not using them.

It is your responsibility as the flyer to make sure you have adequate space for what you are doing. You must allow a clear space downwind of where you're standing at least twice the length of your flying lines to allow for being pulled forward, especially during the launch phase, and a similar amount of space to each side. If people come too close or stand under the kite(s) while you're flying you must fly your kite to a safe place (at the zenith above your head, or land it) and either ask them to move or move yourself

◀ *From top Bullet, Blade III*
▶ *A harness*

until it's safe to fly again. You might want to think about taking out some kind of public indemnity or liability insurance. Many clubs and associations offer this as part of their membership and we recommend that you take out appropriate cover.

There are some other 'contra-indications' for kiting. The kites and flying lines are excellent for 'earthing' lightning so at the first flash of lightning or rumble of thunder get your kite down as fast as possible. Likewise, the kite that dumps itself in the electricity lines will not only fry itself and possibly the flyer, it will quite conceivably short out the national grid and could land you with a hefty fine from the electricity company. It goes without saying that sites next to roads and railways are a complete no-no and anywhere near an airport it is usually prohibited.

All Flexifoil power kites come with full operating instructions and a safety warning notice. Read them well before you take your kite out for the first time. There are some specific safety rules that apply to kiteboarding, buggying and the more extreme activities, which we'll cover in the relevant chapters, but opposite there is a general summary of what you need to do to keep yourself and others safe

One final safety thought before you launch your power kiting career. With the exception of when you're using kites for getting airs, when it's recommended you hang on to the controls at all times, your ultimate safety mechanism is to let go of the control handles or bar completely if you feel that it's all getting too much. The kite will blow downwind and eventually come to ground without the retaining tension on the flying lines. But this really is a final solution and all other efforts should be made to control the kites first. It can present a potentially enormous danger to other kiters or bystanders and means a lot of sorting out of lines and kites to do before you can fly again. Never attempt to stop an escaped kite by grabbing the flying line as it may cut in to your hand. In kiteboarding, where the biggest power is needed, safety systems and leashes are now commonplace so that you can let the kite go and recover it again without risk to yourself or others.

▶ *Blade safety de-power system*

Wind speeds

If you're just starting out with power kites or are just in it for a bit of recreational fun, a simplistic understanding may well be enough. There's either enough wind to fly or not and if there's enough, is there just enough to fly or is it strong enough to make it good fun? In fact it's a popular misconception of our time that you need a roof-lifting wind to fly kites. Normally, most kites will fly well in 10mph or more of wind. If you're getting a bit more specialised and power kiting means getting in your buggy or out on your board as often as possible, then a little more detail will be needed. For instance, you'll almost certainly have more than one size of kite depending on what the wind strength is. In a light wind (10mph) you will need to fly a big kite (a 9.0 m2 Blade II for example) to achieve traction. The same kite in a big wind (20mph+) will be an uncontrollable monster and you'll need less kite to achieve the same power, a 2, 3 or 4 m². It's the same principle as sailing and windsurfing. The more serious you get the more kites you'll have so that you can always maximise. your fun whatever the wind.

All kites come with recommended wind ranges for optimum performance, which you should take good account of. Flying outside those wind ranges might cause damage to your kite or yourself. A set of kites with overlapping wind ranges will cover you for every eventuality.

Kite wind ranges are normally expressed in wind speeds. There are numerous different

ways of measuring speed: Beaufort (Force 1, 2, 3 etc, as on the shipping forecast), miles per hour, kilometres per hour, knots, metres per second. Understanding these and what is the right range for your kite is one thing, actually measuring it on the day you're out flying is another altogether. There are a few ways of doing this. First, watch the weather forecast on television; they usually give forecasted wind speeds (in mph in the UK) in a circle on the chart, with a little arrow attached to show direction. A better and more accurate way would be to buy yourself a pocket wind meter but you'll need to spend a decent amount of money to get something at all accurate. If you're sailing from a centre or club they normally have a high quality anemometer on site giving a constant accurate reading. A less scientific

but nonetheless useful method is to look for wind indicators in the environment; they can give you an enormous amount of information. Watch for smoke or clouds in the sky, flags and trees moving; look at the surface of water for rippling, white horses, waves, etc. Study the table on page 23 which shows all the official measures and a list of indicators you can use.

With time you'll learn to "feel" the wind and make your decision on which kite to use from your experience. You'll know instinctively when to switch to a smaller or bigger kite from your muscle and brain memory of similar situations. One thing you do need to understand is that there's a point at which kiting becomes dangerous however you're doing it. Watch what the serious flyers and riders do. When it gets too big they stay indoors. As a rough guide, anything over Force 6 or 30 mph is going to start making things very exciting to the point of danger and foolhardiness. Over Force 8 or 40 mph and you've only got yourself to blame.

There are a couple of other factors to consider as well. Your flying lines can make a big difference to how the kite performs in different wind speeds. It's all a question of weight, diameter, stretch and the kind of activity you're doing and the drag that results from that combination of factors. Modern power kite flying lines are made of materials that significantly reduce all three factors but you may still be able tweak extra mph of wind range out of your kite by flying on lighter or heavier lines: lighter to generate more power and fly faster, heavier to fly slower and "brake" the kite. Flexifoil power kites suggest in their instructions the appropriate strength flying lines for average and heavy use.

The final thing is the wind direction. It may be a crucial factor if you're a kiteboarder as an offshore (blowing out to sea) wind can result in you being blown away to the danger of the open sea. The main thing to consider though is the smoothness of the wind. Beach sites are great because, often, with an onshore (blowing from the sea) or side wind, the wind is smooth and controlling the kite is much easie, it behaves consistently. An offshore wind will have to come past the land mass and any other obstacles behind. It will be what kiters call lumpy. A lumpy, gusty wind will make the kite fly erratically and, depending on its size, dangerously. Many inland sites have lumpy wind for exactly this

reason. To give you a guide, it usually takes the wind up to seven times the height of the obstacle in lateral distance to smooth itself out again (ergo a 100ft tree or building will have a wind 'shadow' up to 700ft long). Find the most open, exposed site you can and position yourself as far downwind of any obstacles as possible.

▲ Left: Blade III

▲ Right: A wind meter — a very useful gadget

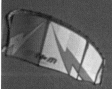

Wind Speed   ## Wind Speed Indicators (probable)

Force	MPH	Knots	KPH	Meter/ Sec	Description	At Sea	On Land
0	<1	<1	<1	0-0.2	Calm	Smooth as glass	Calm; smoke rises vertically
1	1-3	1-3	1-5	0.3-1.5	Light Air	Ripples with no appearance of scales; no foam crests	Smoke drift indicates wind direction; vanes do not move
2	4-7	4-6	6-11	1.6-3.3	Light Breeze	Small wavelets; crests of glassy appearance	Wind felt on face; leaves rustle; vanes begin to move
3	8-12	7-10	12-19	3.4-5.4	Gentle Wind	Large wavelets; crests begin to break, scattered whitecaps	Leaves and small twigs in motion; light flags extended
4	13-18	11-16	20-29	5.5-7.9	Moderate Wind	1-4ft waves; numerous whitecaps	Leaves and loose paper raised up; flags flap; small branches move
5	19-24	17-21	30-38	8.0-10.7	Fresh Wind	4-8ft waves; many whitecaps; some spray	Small trees begin to sway; flags flap and ripple
6	25-31	22-27	39-50	10.8-13.8	Strong Wind	8-13ft waves forming whitecaps everywhere; more spray	Large branches in motion; whistling heard in wires
7	32-38	28-33	51-61	13.9-17.1	Near Gale	13-20ft waves; white foam blown in streaks	Whole trees in motion; resistance felt in walking against wind
8	39-46	34-40	62-74	17.2-20.7	Gale	13-20ft waves; edges of crests beginning to break; foam in streaks	Whole trees in motion; resistance felt in walking against wind (again)
9	47-54	41-47	75-86	20.8-24.4	Strong Gale	20ft waves; sea begins to roll; dense streaks of foam	Slight structural damage occurs; shingles blow from roofs
10	55-63	48-55	87-101	24.5-28.4	Storm	20-30ft waves; white churning sea; rolling is heavy; reduced visibility	Trees broken/uprooted; considerable structural damage occurs

The wind window

Anyone who's come to power kiting from another wind sport might be more familiar with the term 'wind envelope' It's the actual field of manoeuvre described by the kite on the end of its flying lines as it moves around the sky with the flyer standing still and it dictates how much and what type of power your wing will generate. Try for yourself, there's a limit to each side of you and how far over your head that you can fly the kite before it either stops moving or loses power, stalls and falls out of the sky or both. With you as a fixed point at its centre the wind window described resembles the surface of a quarter sphere. There really isn't any kite that can make the full quarter sphere requiring a full 180 degree lateral pass, more like 130 to 140 degrees as an average. The illustration opposite will help you understand. Bear in mind that the wind, especially light wind, can shift and change direction. Your orientation shifts with the wind until you relocate the new window centre and edges. On a beach site wind shift could well be associated with the tides and a flat calm day can easily turn into a real hoolie following a tide change.

Traditionally, sport and power kites are most efficient when they are at the centre of the wind window flying horizontally across the sky at roughly head height or slightly above. Here they move fastest and pull hardest. Keep flying horizontally and the kite will gradually slow down and lose power as it reaches the edge of its window.

Turn the kite round and fly back across the wind window. As you reach the centre turn upwards and fly the kite straight up the wind window. If the wind is strong enough you'll notice yourself being pulled by a rush of power followed by the same slowing down and de-powering effect until the kite reaches a 'parked' position up above your head. This is known as the zenith or 'safety' position. There's almost no power in the kite up here and it's the place to try and steer the kite if you ever feel you're getting into difficulties.

Flying a big power kite near the centre of the window will generate enormous lateral pull and this is where you'll find yourself leaning right back, even lying down, to stop yourself being pulled over and dragged along on your front. In fact you rarely see buggy drivers or kiteboarders fly their big kites near centre window because the lateral pull would be too much to hold, leading to a big horizontal wipe out. What they do is to use a different part of the wind window to generate the kind of power that is most useful to them. As with wind speeds, it is something that is worth understanding in principle but will become much more intuitive with experience. Your skill as a flyer will be in learning how to manipulate the kite in the wind window to deliver the kind and quantity of pull you want. Generally speaking, lighter wind means a smaller (narrower and lower) wind window in which the kite will be moving much slower. You'll need to 'work' it near the edges, even in centre window, to achieve real power, whereas in a big wind you'll find

that the kite has a bigger wind window, is much faster (not least because smaller kites always fly faster) and has strong pull over a much bigger area of the window.

▲ Kite in the parked position

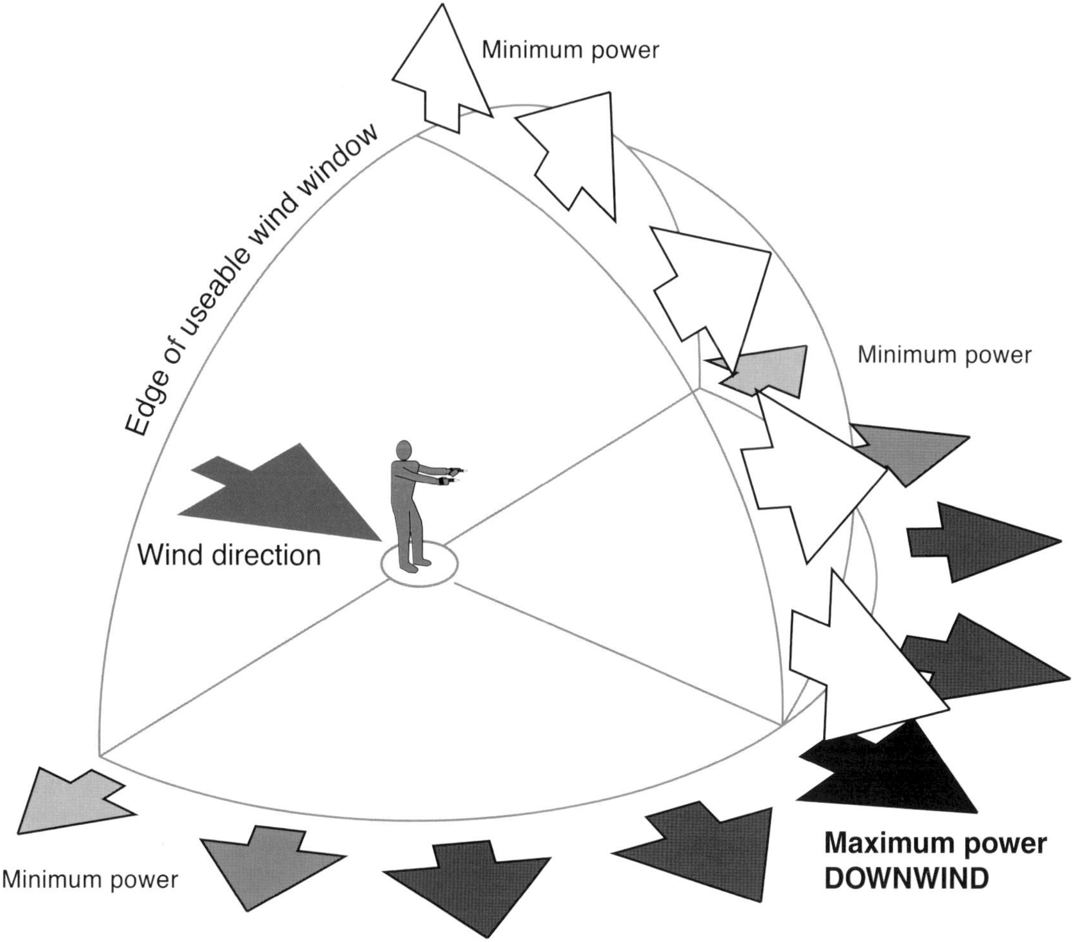

Minimum power

Minimum power

Edge of useable wind window

Wind direction

Minimum power

Maximum power DOWNWIND

Two Line
Power Kites
for land use

"These are great starter or recreational kites on which you can learn the basic skills and add to them. They're a sociable kite because friends can join kites together for a bigger pull."

Andreya Wharry
Professional kiteboarder and power kite instructor

2

The Flexifoil Stacker 6', Proteam 8', Super 10' and recreational flying

YOU COULD SAY that anyone who's not a pro board rider or buggy driver is a recreational flyer, many just out for the pure fun, not too worried about developing their flying skills and not too concerned about getting onto a board or into a buggy. If you're the kind of person who likes to keep your kites in the car to use occasionally, when there's a good wind blowing, you're a recreational flyer. If, on the other hand, you like to get out as often as possible with the biggest rig that's appropriate for the conditions, with the added spice of big jumps, fast buggying or carving up the surf, then you're an altogether different beast.

Most people trying power kiting for the first time or starting to fly regularly do indeed start on a Flexifoil power kite. For many people the first step is going out with a friend who's already converted to kite power and having a go on theirs. The second step normally comes the day afterwards when you hunt down your nearest power kite dealer (there's a list of recommended Flexifoil dealers available at www.flexifoil.com) and buy yourself one because, like 99.9% of first timers, you're an instant convert. If your ultimate aim is to take power kiting to its limits then it's perfectly possible to learn kite skills on one of the big traction wings but you can learn more, much quicker, if you start with one of these fantastic sky-sweeping two-line Flexifoil kites. On its 40 metre lines it really fills up the sky, moving fast and pulling hard and few other kites are able to describe the shape and extent of the wind window as well as a Flexi. Its distinctive shape has made it a household name among kite flyers the world over. Instantly recognisable individually or in the big stacks serious Flexi freaks love so much, it is the face that launched a thousand crazy power kiting pastimes.

The 6' Stacker was of course Flexifoil's first ever design and its enduring popularity speaks volumes for what a great invention it was, or rather is. How many other extreme sports products can make the same claim that, relatively unchanged from the original concept, they've been bestsellers for more than 25 years? What makes the Stacker so great is that it's easy to fly, it's fast, it's almost unbreakable and it gives you a taste of what real kite power can feel like without it ever getting too much. It's even the choice of top clergy, the late and very reverend John Habgood, former Archbishop of York, a well-publicised Flexifoil fanatic who evidently used his for some sinfully good sessions.

When you're ready you can switch to the slower moving but heavier pulling bigger kites, the 8' or 10' 'grunt' versions. The increase in pull through the wingspans is impressive and with a Super 10' flying in 15 mph of good steady wind you'll be getting one of the best workouts you've had in ages. The Proteam 8' is the compromise kite. Fast through the air like a Stacker, plenty of pull like a Super 10 to exercise your muscles. And even if you do progress to far more serious power kiting extremes you'll still keep your old Flexis in your kite bag because for pure fun and recreational flying little can beat these first three members of the Flexifoil family.

▶ A stack of powered-up Proteam 8s

◀ A stack of 6' Stackers

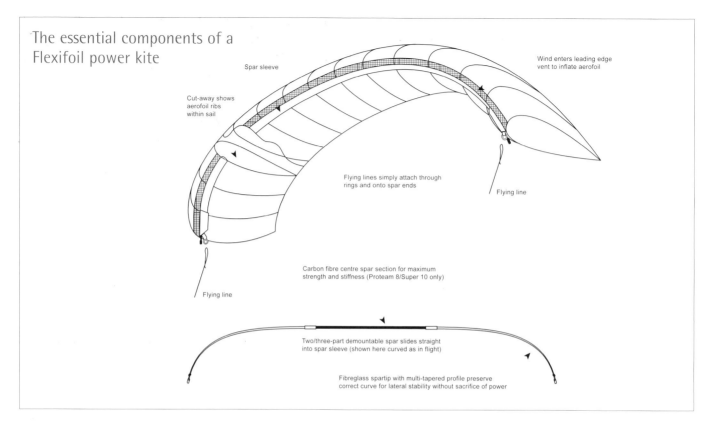

The essential components of a Flexifoil power kite

Spar sleeve

Cut-away shows aerofoil ribs within sail

Wind enters leading edge vent to inflate aerofoil

Flying lines simply attach through rings and onto spar ends

Flying line

Carbon fibre centre spar section for maximum strength and stiffness (Proteam 8/Super 10 only)

Flying line

Two/three-part demountable spar slides straight into spar sleeve (shown here curved as in flight)

Fibreglass spartip with multi-tapered profile preserve correct curve for lateral stability without sacrifice of power

Descriptions and uses

"Simplicity has helped it remain a popular recreational power kite but its efficiency and reliability, like all functioning designs, depends on a combination of good conception, suitable materials and quality workmanship."

Andrew Jones
Flexifoil co-designer

Time to get technical again and take a close look at these basic Flexifoil kite wings and what makes them tick.

The Flexifoil Stacker was the first and original modern power kite. Although there have been changes of materials used, its construction today is basically the same kite as the original concept.

It is best described as an aerofoil kite or wing. It's similar in basic structure to a modern rectangular parachute or parapente. The kite is essentially two rectangular sheets of fabric held together lengthways and sepa-

rated to give it a three-dimensional shape by a series of ribs between the two. This shape is critical as it dictates the amount of lift or pull delivered. The ribs divide the kite wing into sections called cells. Another way of looking at it is to say that the wing consists of a series of cells joined together. The kite is sealed at the rear (trailing) edge but the front (leading) edge has a gauze opening to allow the kite to inflate, which it does under wind pressure. Once inflated the kite has an aerofoil profile, that is to say, in cross section it is similar to a conventional aeroplane wing, fat at the front

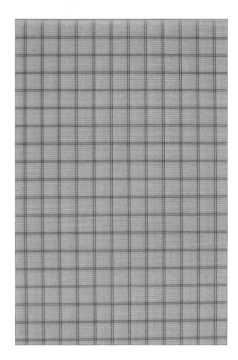

edge tapering to a point at the back. Take a look at the diagram opposite. It's like an aeroplane wing and, just like an aeroplane wing, it's the difference in speed of airflow over the two surfaces of the wing leading to a corresponding difference in air pressure that generates the power and forward movement (or lift in the case of the plane).

Those of you who've had a look at a parapente or a parachute will be familiar with the complex structure of "shroud" lines coming from points all over the underside surface of the wing. These usually join together at two points, one on each side of the wing,

Super 10' with two lines
Close-up of ripstop Chikara

and these two points are what the pilot's harness attaches to, usually hanging a little way below on two extension lines. All that string and the need to keep it in good order can be a daunting prospect but a very necessary one as these wings have no frame and require a structure of shroud lines to maintain their shape in flight. Otherwise it collapses in on itself becoming a flightless piece of cloth in the sky.

Ordinarily a soft aerofoil kite needs a similar structure and many of the big traction wings that we'll be looking at later are exactly that kind. But the beauty of the Flexifoil idea is its simplicity (almost accidentally achieved as Jones and Merry were unaware of other soft aerofoil wings with complex shroud lines already developed), there's very little that can go wrong. Instead of a complex shroud or 'bridle' (in kitespeak) the kite has a single flexible rod that fits into a pocket that runs across the leading edge of the kite and keeps the sail spread out in the correct shape to fly. The rod also helps the kite self-adjust its angle of attack against the wind, pivoting around the spar in different areas of the wind window and under different degrees of power. The sail tips and the control lines are attached to the tips of this rod. Once inflated and with the tension of the control lines fixed to you, the flyer, the kite has an uncontrollable need to move forwards and it is up to you to pilot it around the sky.

The rod itself is a two-piece fibreglass rod with a brass ferrule connector at the centre. This connector has plastic grips to prevent the rod sections popping apart in flight. It also has the correct combination of strength, weight and flexibility that the kite's performance requires. As much as any other factor, the rod's strong, stiff centre and flexible tips give the kite its classic arched shape in the sky. The curve or arch of the kite is another critical factor in its functioning.

The sail material used on early prototype Stackers was plastic sheet which wasn't really up to the job and a new fabric was quickly identified that gave the kites the durability necessary for commercial success, one that is still in use today. Sail-cloth nylon as used on yachting sails, known as 'ripstop', was the obvious choice, really, having all the qualities required to complete the Flexifoil formula: lightweight, tough, durable, low

stretch. Ripstop comes in many grades or weights and for kites the lightest one was selected, spinnaker nylon. In time kite industry demands were great enough that fabric manufacturers began to make ripstop specifically for kites. All Flexifoil kites (6, 8 and 10) are now made from Chikara ripstop nylon, specifically designed for kite manufacture. The excellent colour ranges available mean that there's good choice of kite colours available and Flexifoil kites look great, an important consideration as hopefully you're going to spend a lot of time looking at them up in the sky.

The bigger, Proteam 8 and Super 10, kites use the same basic design and materials with some modifications. Where the Stacker has

▲ A young flyer enjoying his Flexifoil

▶ Top: Stacker 6'

▶ Bottom: Spar in its spar pocket

ten cells across its span, the Proteam has 14 and the Super 10 18. This affects something called the 'aspect ratio': the ratio of the depth to the span. Lower aspect ratios (the Stacker) tend to be more stable, higher aspect ratios (the Super 10) more efficient. The sails of the two bigger kites are made from ripstop nylon but the front rod is different, using the fibreglass sections at the tips with a solid, carbon fibre rod in the centre. The combination of ultra-stiff carbon and flexible fibreglass give these bigger kites the same arched shape in flight as the Stacker.

Flown singly or in stacks, Flexifoils are ideal for learning how to handle power kites and can be used for taking your first steps in kite traction: body dragging, getting airs, etc. It's possible to use stacked Flexifoils for buggying but by no means as easy as if you use one of the kites designed specifically for that. Although an adult toy recommended for ages 12 and upwards, children under 12 are perfectly capable of flying them (kids often learn much faster than adults) but will need supervision in case the kite starts to pull too much. For sheer speed through the sky, nothing can beat a Flexifoil Stacker, and that's official. 110mph has been clocked, a figure you're very welcome to try and surpass. The Proteam takes you to the realm of kite traction, enough to start pulling an average build person around. The Super 10 is the undisputed bestselling power kite in the world. Awesome power, steady in flight, easy control, it's the kite to test your skill and muscles to the maximum.

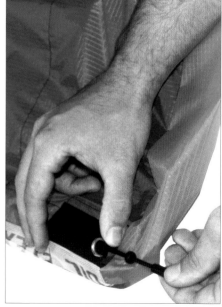

Setting up and packing up procedures

When you buy your first Flexifoil kite it will come in a storage bag, an instruction and safety manual, flying lines, control wrist straps, a product registration card, a Flexifoil sticker and a one month free repair card. If any of these items are missing contact your local dealer or Flexifoil direct. You are thoroughly recommended to take the whole thing home, read the instruction and safety manual, put the kite together and take it apart at least once in the calm of your living room before you head off to your nearest flying site for a blast. Standing in a windy field trying to read the manual and control the flapping nylon sail at the same time is not conducive to happy power kiting. Reading the instructions you'll become aware of how simple these kites are to prepare for action. A quick runthrough confirms it. Follow the instructions and you can't really go wrong. And if you do, take the kite back to your local dealer for some advice.

With the kite fully assembled it's time to head back to your equipment bag for your flying or control lines and handles or wrist straps. First, take the flying lines. There are two lines packed together on one line winder and they're ready to use with a 'sleeved' loop on each end of each line.

The quality of the lines you use can make a

huge difference to the efficiency, response and general flying of the kite. Nowadays all power kite manufacturers recommend using a hi-tech flying line such as Spectra or Dyneema to get the best performance from your kite. Both are synthetic fibres. Spectra was developed as part of the American space exploration programme and Dyneema is a similar product made in Europe. Dyneema flying lines are strong, lightweight, low diameter, have less than 5% stretch and are very slippery. They enable kites to fly efficiently with minimal drag and once flown in (a few hours of flying pulls any remaining stretch out) give a 'fly by wire' feel of immediate response. Conventional nylon or polyester lines are heavier, fatter and have up to 20% stretch. Flexifoil-recommended line packs are always Dyneema. Their slipperiness

▲ *Straps around a ground stake*

▶ *A Super 10*

means you can fly easily with multiple twists in the lines. Their chemical make-up gives them a low melting point and explains the need for a Dacron sleeve at each end, where the knots are tied.

To attach the kite:

- unwind a few metres of both lines, separate them and take one end to each kite tip.
- put the looped end of line through the metal ring at the sail tip and pull a little excess line through with it.
- now make a lark's head knot in the looped end, as shown opposite in our step by step instructions (this is the single most useful knot in power kiting so learn it now).
- place the lark's head knot between the grommet and end cap on the spar and pull it tight, as shown in your instructions.
- then pull the excess line back out through the metal ring towards your wrist straps; this was only necessary to have sufficient line to tie the knot.

Once you've unwound the lines you're ready for the flying straps, which attach with the same lark's head knot as before, although it's achieved in a slightly different way:

- take the looped end of your flying line and pass it through the metal ring on the end of the straps and then pull the strap through the loop (see step by step instructions).
- pull it tight and the lark's head will form itself around the metal ring.

▸ *How to make a lark's head knot*

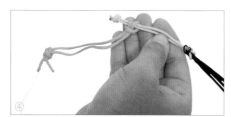

The great thing about the lark's head is that it's a slip knot. The more you pull the tighter it locks so there's no chance of it coming undone in flight. But as soon as the tension is released (after landing the kite) it's relatively easy to pull loose and undo.

How to launch, fly and land

"My advice to anyone starting out in power kiting: never ever underestimate the power of the wind and respect the elements to the full, keep the wind at your back and GO BIG!".

Jason Furness
Flexifoil team kiteboarder and tester

Launching the kite

Launching can be achieved on your own or with assistance. Let's look at the assisted launch first:

- position yourself so that the kite is as directly downwind of you as possible with your flying lines attached and untwisted and the appropriate line going to each hand. Adopt a good body position, hands in the handlebar position, just in front of your torso, arms slightly bent and elbows tucked in, knees slightly flexed ready for the kite to launch and start pulling.
- your helper should hold the kite in the centre of its leading edge by the spar which they will feel through the pocket, making sure that the kite is the right way up (gauze

opening above the spar) and taking care not to block the vents with their hand. Have them hold the kite above their head and wait for it to fully inflate.

- when you're sure the kite's ready and there's enough wind, call to your helper to release the kite. They should not try to throw the kite into the air. The kite should fly out of their hand, straight up the wind window. In lighter wind the flyer may need to take a few steps backward at the moment of launch to help the kite up into the stronger air currents. Avoid lifting your hands and arms to encourage the kite to climb as this actually makes controlling the kite more difficult; keep your elbows tucked into your sides ready to start steering.

We'll look at steering in a moment but first let's quickly run through solo launching.

There are two ways of doing this, both requiring a bit of preparation of the kite:

- the first way: lay the kite right way up on the ground but at an angle, not straight on to the wind but less than perpendicular, as shown in the diagram. When you pull the kite straight by pulling gently on the line attached to the furthest tip, it will inflate and get ready to lift off.
- the second way (which may be better in very strong wind) is to lay the kite down at an angle to the wind as before, but upside down (gauze below the spar). This time you will need a sharp pull on the furthest tip to

▸ *Top: Assisted launch*
▸ *Bottom: Two solo launch techniques*

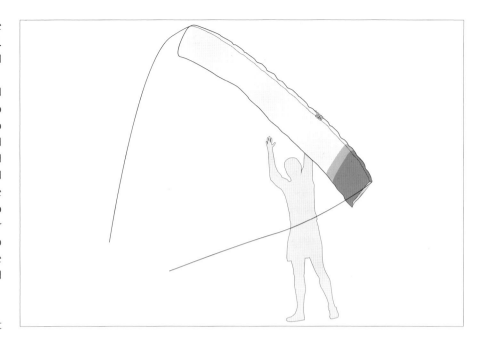

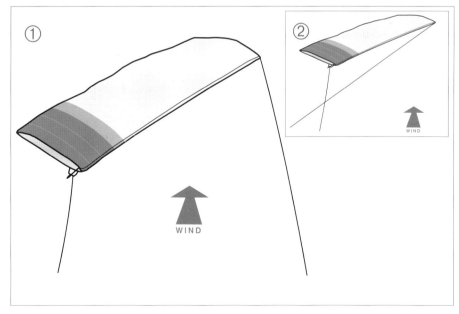

flip the kite over so it can inflate.

- whichever way you get the kite into the correct position, once it's inflated you will probably need to walk smoothly backwards a few paces to get it to lift off. Avoid hard tugging; this impedes launch.

Like anything, practice makes perfect so persevere if you don't get it straight off. Once the kite is inflated you should follow the same procedure as for the assisted launch. Normally the kite should lift off on its own but you may need to help it up the first few feet. Don't jerk with your arms; pull back by walking steadily and smoothly backwards. Losing a few metres backwards is no problem as, all being well, you're going to be pulled forwards again once the kite's flying. If it doesn't launch fairly quickly go and set it up and try again. Dragging the kite across the ground too much is a sure way of damaging it. Use the assisted launch if needed.

Steering the kite

If you can steer a bike or a car you can fly a power kite. The main thing is to keep your movements as smooth as possible and avoid steering jerkily. When you launch the kite it will fly straight up the sky (if this doesn't happen check the troubleshooting section which follows). You can either wait until it reaches a hover or parked position above your head to start steering it (you'll have to watch out that you don't over-fly and drop the kite out of the sky) or preferably take control of it before it reaches the top of the wind window, thereby keeping it moving, the thing Flexis like best. Remember that the

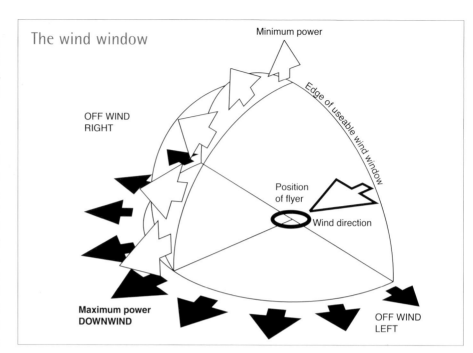

The wind window

Minimum power

OFF WIND RIGHT

Edge of useable wind window

Position of flyer

Wind direction

Maximum power DOWNWIND

OFF WIND LEFT

stronger the wind the quicker the kite flies and the faster your reactions will need to be. Try in a moderate wind first unless or until you're feeling really confident:

- as the kite reaches three-quarters of the way up the wind window, pull back a short distance, smoothly and firmly on the right line. The kite flies to the right.
- pull similarly on the left line; the kite flies to the left.
- bring your hands parallel and the kite flies straight up the wind window to a hover (the zenith position).

You can spend a bit of time moving backwards and forwards across the sky like that if

you like but it's more interesting to start doing some loops:

- pull on the right line, this time keeping the pull going so that the kite flies to the right and then describes a circle downwards to the right. Don't pull the kite into a really tight spin which tends to 'stall' the kite, a wider, smooth loop is good, enough to bring the kite round in a complete loop, the bottom of which should be a good few metres above the ground. A combined pull with the right and push with the left, just like on a bike, makes the smoothest turn. Keep pulling on the right line until the kite comes round and it's pointing straight up at the window again.

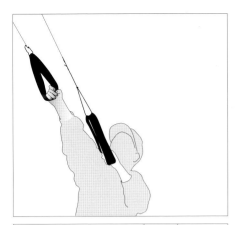

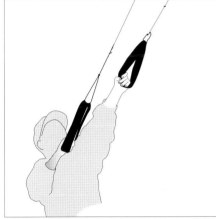

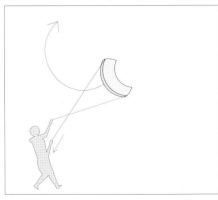

- as the kite comes round full circle and is pointing straight up the wind window, bring your hands parallel with each other and it will fly straight up.

At this point your lines are twisted round each other but don't worry, it makes almost no difference to the controls of the kite. Don't cross your hands to compensate, to untwist the lines all you need to do is:

- pull on the left line hard and long enough to bring the kite round in a complete loop to the left at the end of which, if you bring your hands parallel, it should be once again pointing straight up the wind window, roughly in the centre.

▲ *The beach – an excellent place to fly*

◄ *Top: Left turn*

◄ *Middle: Right turn*

◄ *Bottom: Lines crossing and wrapping*

- as the kite comes up the wind window again it's up to you, right or left, and so on:

From this point on the freedom of the sky is yours. You can start to play with wider and tighter loops and spins, explore the wind window and get to grips with the big lateral pull low down. The best bet to begin with is to keep flying right and left loops, a figure of eight on its side, which gives you a nice continuous pattern you can fly whilst you really familiarise yourself with how the kite handles. You can fly quite a few loops in one direction before you need to untwist but you will need to at some point. Try to keep a rough count in your head and untwist from time to time.

Flexifoils are very, very durable, which is just as well because almost certainly you'll have some big wipe-outs to begin with, crashing the kites hard into the ground. It's a big laugh, specially when someone else does

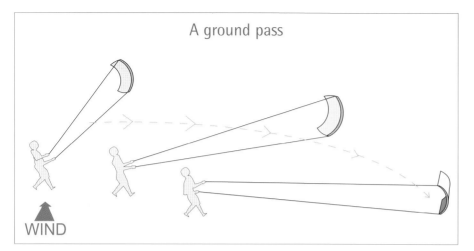

A ground pass

WIND

it, but try and keep your crashes to a mini-mum as repeated 'unintentional ground contacts' will surely damage the kite eventually.

One other manoeuvre you will certainly want to try is a horizontal pass or sweep which, with practice, you'll be able to make closer and closer to the ground. Let's start with a right to left sweep:

- pull on the right line as if to do a big right loop taking the kite down to the bottom quarter of the wind window.
- now it's all a question of timing and may take a few goes to get it right. Instead of completing the loop, when the kite is pointing across the wind window bring your hands almost parallel, right hand slightly above the left, and fly the kite across the wind window from right to left.
- as the kite starts to slow down on the left side of the window, pull again on your right line so the kite turns until it's pointing across the window, going back the way it

came. Bring your hands almost parallel again but with the left above the right and fly a pass back the other way.

Simply reverse the above swapping left for right to fly it in the opposite direction. Soon you'll be confident enough to try those impressive ground-skimming passes, always watching out for other fliers and stray passers by, of course.

Landing the kite

Sooner or later you're going to get tired, especially if you're flying a Proteam 8 or Super 10, and want to land the kite or pass it on to someone else. In the latter case it's very simple. Fly your kite up to top centre of the window, the 'park' position, slip your wrists out of the straps and pass them over to the next flyer. But, even so, sooner or later you'll still need to land. Do not fly a fully inflated

and powered-up kite straight into the ground as it may well burst the sail, there's a safe and simple way to do it. See opposite page:

- put the kite into a horizontal pass as described, low down if you can but that will come with practice.
- as the kite passes centre window and starts flying towards the edge, keep it going in that direction.
- the kite slows down and the pull reduces until eventually the kite flies out of the wind window and falls gently to the ground. You can take a step or two forwards to make sure it settles on the ground if you like.

The kite will normally land upside down. Although it can't take off from that position you should still immobilise it. If it's not upside down go and put it that way. If you're just landing for a rest, a very good idea is to use a ground stake or peg for your straps. That way your kites can't blow away in a big gust and it will help keep your flying lines in good order. Most good kite shops sell ground stakes but at a push a big tent peg will do the trick. A non-abrasive weighted item such as a carry bag or water bottle makes a good kite weight.

Congratulations, you're now an accomplished power kite flyer. Practise your controls to left and right until you're confident on both sides and you'll soon be ready to graduate to the serious stuff. That could be flying big stacks or moving on to the big traction wings for buggying and kiteboarding. Either way, you'll be joining very good

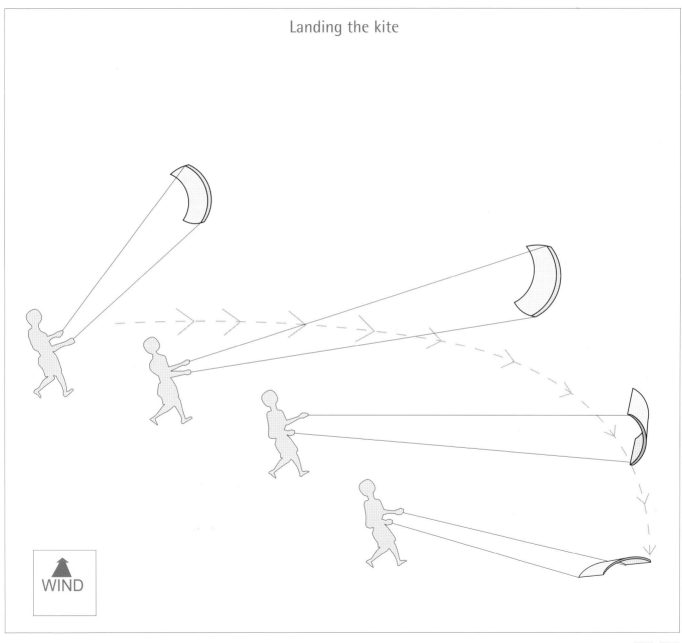

WIND

company as one of the many satisfied Flexifoil kite owners.

Troubleshooting

It's worth repeating that the beauty of the Flexifoil concept is its simplicity, there's very little that can go wrong. Nevertheless, you may find that your kite doesn't seem to be flying properly. Check the following :

The power kite flies continually to one side:

1. Check that both lines are the same length. The best way to do this is to peg the loops at one end to the ground and pull them tight from the other. A quick visual check will show you. If they're unequal you will need to make an adjustment. Undo the loop of the longest line and undo the knots holding the line sleeving in place. Slide the sleeving along until it is equal with the shorter line and retie the knots.

2. Check that you and the kite are correctly positioned in the centre of the wind window. If the kite is near the edge it will want to fly towards the centre as soon as it launches.

The power kite 'bounces' violently in flight after launching:

1. There may be sand or water inside the cells. Land the kite and try and remove the sand through the gauze vent.

2. The sail may be very wet (affects smaller models mostly). Dry the sail thoroughly before relaunching.

▸ *Top: Dyneema line*
▸ *Far right: Damaged kite*

The wingtips 'flap' during flight:

1. The sail may be over-stretched on the spar. Move the line attachments one to four centimetres further in. This may require moving and resticking the grommet or stopper (super glue is recommended). Flapping for long periods will eventually damage the fabric.

2. The fabric may be worn or damaged.

If it's anything other than the above, go straight back to your dealer or contact Flexifoil International direct. It could be a fault with the kite but it could also be a simple mistake you're making.

The kites are guaranteed against faulty manufacture but not against faulty flying. Kites may well end up getting damaged and

Flexifoil run an excellent and reasonably priced repair service, which you can use via your dealer or direct. Small-hole repairs can be done yourself with a repair kit. Larger tears should be sent for repair straight away. Check your kite over regularly and get repairs done quickly. Check the spar sections too, the carbon centre sections for the Proteam 8 and Super 10 should not be roughly handled as they can easily chip and weaken if knocked against other spar sections. Running without a repair is inviting bigger trouble later. And you'll have to face the fact that if you really hammer your kite, flying day in day out for long periods, especially in bright sunlight with its harmful ultra violet rays, it (the sail fabric primarily) is going to wear out completely one day.

Stacking

Stacking is the most common term given to linking together and simultaneous flying of two or more stunt, sport or power kites on one set of control lines (also known as flying in 'train'). Different sized Flexifoils can be stacked together although it works better with equal-sized kites. If you do decide to stack different sizes put the smallest kite at the front (nearest the flyer) for the best performance.

There are two main reasons for wanting to stack kites, particularly power kites and especially Flexifoils. The first reason is that by adding to the first kite you are increasing the pull on the end of your lines and hence the range of stuff you can do. There's a rough formula for working out by how much you increase pull, assuming you're using same-sized kites. When you add a second kite you virtually double the pull. Adding a third adds half as much pull as the first two. A fourth will add about a third of that, and so on. The point is that the pull increases to the extent that, should you decide for some reason to want to fly a stack of 208 Stackers, as Flexifoil did at the Le Touquet kite festival in 1993, you'll need three bulldozers to anchor the stack and three people heaving on each line to turn it round in the sky. Get together with a few mates and you can soon have some serious traction going. You'll need friends anyway because when you're flying big stacks in a decent wind you soon get

▸ Stacking

tired and you can pass the stack on to someone else while you laugh at them being dragged all over the field.

Power kite pull is almost impossible to quantify in terms of things like pounds per square inch or barr, especially with the wind being such a variable factor. What is relatively clear is that you can roughly gauge how the kites pull in relation to each other, even in stacks. Roughly speaking, two Stackers are equal to one Proteam and three Stackers to one Super 10. Two Proteams are equivalent to four Stackers and three Proteams to two Super 10s. Three Super 10s are equivalent to a big nine stack of Stackers.

The other main reason for stacking is that it looks brilliant, that goes for the flyer and

anyone watching. With half a dozen kites stacked you've got a big and colourful object sweeping majestically around the sky. Looking at your kites, feeling the pull and power and knowing that you are in control, is an immensely satisfying experience, especially if you know that at any moment you could switch that power to max for some extremely radical fun. Follow the instructions for stacking kites together in your instruction manual. There are two ways suggested and either will do the trick very nicely. Accuracy is all important as any slight differences in stacking lengths will result in the stack not flying correctly, if at all. And there's a formula for the correct distance between stacked kites: roughly two-thirds of the length of the leading edge. So for two Stackers you would need about 4' stacking lines. Flexifoil make it easy to build up your stack, selling 'add-on' kites, minus the control lines and straps but including a ready-made stacking line kit which requires nothing more complicated than lark's head knots to attach.

With additional kites attached you're ready to launch your stack. This too can be done solo or assisted. For the solo launch you should use the first method for solo launching a single kite; laying the kites the right way up at an angle to the wind and pulling them round gently with the flying lines when you're ready to launch. The kites normally inflate and lift off themselves but you may need to take some smooth, steady steps back to get them up. Do not jerk with your arms and don't persist in dragging the kites if they don't launch.

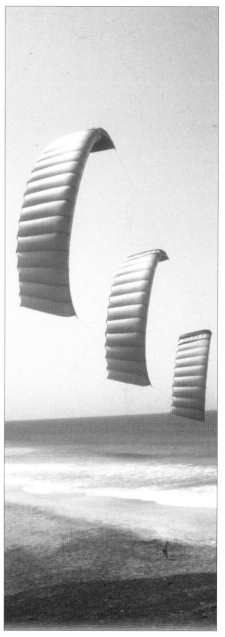

For an assisted launch your helper should hold the rear kite of the stack, holding by the spar in the usual way. Once all the kites in the stack are inflated, launch as for one kite.

In flight the stack should, if all your setting up and measuring is correct, 'lock' into position. If it doesn't and the kites are always 'shuffling' or simply not flying there are a few things you can check:

▲ *A four stack of Stacker 6s*
▶ *6/8/10 Flexifoils being stacked*
◀ *Top: A three stack of Stacker 6's*
◀ *Bottom: Stacking off the beach*

- make sure all the kites are attached the right way up.
- check that the stacking lines or loops are measured accurately.
- adjust the attachment points of a kite that seems to be lagging back, as you would for a single kite with flapping wingtips.
- try moving a problem kite to a different position in the stack or swapping its spar with another kite.

Whichever way you decide to build your stack you will need to check your stacking lines (and indeed your flying lines) regularly for wear and tear. The force and friction generated is considerable. Replace any that are worn or damaged straight away.

When the stack is flying smoothly you will immediately feel the extra power and notice that the stack flies slower than a single kite. The more kites you add, the slower it flies. And the stronger it pulls. It's very important that you are aware of the strength and maximum load of your flying lines. The recommended strength for a single kite will normally be sufficient for a stack of two kites the same size. Any more than that and you will need to get some stronger lines or risk a line breaking just when you didn't want it to, heavily powered up and getting into a skid or jump. The extra lifting power of the stack will more than compensate any extra weight of the lines. Consult your local dealer or Flexifoil International who will be happy to advise you. Then you're ready for some more serious power kite action.

Skidding

Skidding or skudding and body dragging are the first ways most people discover the hidden joys of power kiting. Even if eventually you're heading for a kiteboard and the wide blue yonder, you've got to learn how to fly kites and you're going to learn skidding as part of your basic training. Skidding and getting airs require even more flying space so make sure you've got plenty of room downwind of where you're flying to allow movement forwards.

▶ Skidding

The general idea is to generate enough consistent pull from the stack to tow you along, usually on your feet or on your back, although you can try body surfing in shallow water on your front. You'll be aware that if you keep flying big figure eights with your kite(s) they gain and lose power in relation to their position in the wind window. What you'll need to do to go skidding any distance is keep the kites powered up for long enough to move you along. Here's how it goes:

• steer the kites up the centre of the wind window and begin a right-hand loop. You can try it in the opposite direction by substituting left for right if you like.

• as the kites come round their loop towards the centre of the wind window they will begin to power up. Get your feet flat on the ground and lean back to resist being pulled over on your front. You should feel yourself starting to move forward.

• keep your shoulders back and your body in a straight line if possible, leaning backwards, shoulders behind hips behind feet. As the kite hits centre window about half way up, pull it into a tighter loop to keep it turning in the centre window thereby keeping it fully powered up. Too tight a spin will lose power so you may need a few goes to get it just right. Keep your body position and try to go with the kite, releasing the grip of your feet slightly until you're accelerating forwards.

• after a few turns you may need to reverse the direction of the kite to untwist your lines but you'll want to keep the power on.

Keep the kites roughly in centre window and keep leaning back and sliding forward on the flats of your feet and back.

• you can 'switch the power off' at almost any time by flying the kites upwards, out of centre window (or out to one edge). Fly the kites up to the park position, stand up and walk back to your starting point to have another go.

Beaches are great for skidding: hard, flat sand for speed; soft sand for really digging the feet in and 'skiing' along. Inland sites are ok too but you'll have a bumpier ride. From personal experience I can thoroughly recommend a grassy playing field, recent rain and plastic waterproof trousers for one of the fastest skids you can get. Make sure you're properly kitted-out wherever you're going to fly. Decent ankle-supporting footwear, sweat shirt and pants to prevent scratching or grazing on the ground, even a crash helmet, wrist guards and knee pads may be necessary depending on the conditions and the size of your stack. With practice you'll be able to pull some amazing skids and have skid mark competitions with your mates and the longest skid wins.

Getting airs

Otherwise known as kite jumping or moonwalking, getting airs is where power kiting really departs from normal ground-based kiting and turns into an exercise in antigravity and weightlessness. You may have seen other people getting air, down at your

"The first jumps I started doing were a real buzz,
as with most people the first wasn't intentional! A little bit of knowledge is dangerous
and you keep pushing things until Mother Nature kicks you up the arse."

Andreya Wharry,
Professional kiteboarder and power kite instructor

local beach or flying field or on some power kiting or extreme sport vid down at your local store. You may well have experienced kite jumping inadvertently during your flying and skidding stage but either way there's probably going to come a time when you want to see what it's like to get air born kite-style.

The first thing to say is that you cannot use kites to fly in the same way as a parachute or parapente so please don't try. Nevertheless, now you really are going to have to think about some personal protection. The boots, helmets and pads are much more necessary. There are many stories, including one about someone in England 'flying' a river estuary, of jumpers picking up a secondary gust once up in the air and ending up in a vastly different jump situation from the one they'd envisaged a few seconds before. Kite jumping can be a real ankle and wrist snapper with all those heavy landings, especially in the learning phase. Expect the unexpected and, above all, show proper respect for what you're doing. Even small jumps need big power and if things go wrong under those circumstances you could end up in serious difficulty.

It seems obvious that, with jumping, what you're looking for is lift rather than lateral pull. In fact a basic maxim is to concentrate on getting altitude and the wind speed will take care of distance. This means you must not bring the kites too low down in the wind window or you'll simply end up going for a facial scrape down the field. The kites must

◀ *A jumper with a stack of Super 10's*

▶ *Getting air*

stay higher in the window which means you never use their full power. That's why you need a lot more kite up in the sky to get you air born and that's why it becomes that bit more dangerous.

The ideal kite for getting airs will have fast acceleration to haul you up in the air and will be a two-line kite to reduce its manoeuvrability. If you use a four-line kite you will need to be very careful as their extra manoeuvrability and strong acceleration are harder to control because of the brake-line effect. Stacks of Flexis or single large traction kites specifically designed for jumping are the best option. Whichever you use you will be dealing with a huge amount of kite power.

You will need to resist the kites' pull for as long as possible until the moment of release, levering against them as the power builds up for the jump. On a beach you can even dig a hole to give you a wall to lever against. When the moment comes and you let go for your jump, everything happens very quickly and there's a lot of energy involved, your own and the kites'. Jumping with five Super 10s in a 20mph wind means there's about 3 Gs of force on your body as you leave the ground. You're going to need to be reasonably fit and not easily breakable. It's probably not a good idea to start off at that level. Start small and work your way up. It won't be long before you're counting the seconds of flight and measuring your jumps in tens of metres. Discretion is very much the part of valour in power kiting, however, and you shouldn't be embarrassed about stopping if conditions and the size or height of the jumps get too much.

How to jump:

- steer the kite(s) up to the park position at the top centre or zenith of the wind window. Get ready to brace your body and find a good 'lever' position. Without pulling the kites into a full loop, steer them across and down one edge of the wind window until they're about half way up or down the wind window pointing slightly towards the edge. This is done with a small pull on either the right or left line. It's common to feel more confident setting a jump up from one side than the other so try both and see which feels best.
- now pull slightly with the opposite hand to point the kites in towards the window centre. They will accelerate and pick up power very quickly. Keep leaning back and levering with your body. In lighter winds you may find that running in the opposite direction from that which the kites are moving will help 'crank' up the power.
- as the kites approach centre window, roughly halfway up, steer them so they fly straight up the wind window. At the same time you can release your resistance to the kite and will feel yourself pulled, jerked off the ground arms first, up into the sky, legs trailing behind you. Hold on tight and enjoy the weightless moment.
- watch the ground as it rushes up to meet you for touch down and swing your feet and legs forward pendulum style so you can land on your feet or back.
- once you've hit the ground again you can recover control of the kites. They should be flying up near the top of the wind window with little pull.

- pick yourself up and, keeping the kites up at the zenith, you can go back for another go. Either that or try and crawl to your mobile phone to call an ambulance.

There's another way of generating lift that doesn't require levering against the kites' pull: you execute the same manoeuvre as for light winds. As you bring the kites across the window to initiate the jump, run in the opposite direction from the kites' direction of travel, remembering to steer the kites up the window at the appropriate moment. This creates leverage and whips you up into the air as the kites power up and drive up the wind window.

Make sure you're really confident before you try and hit any really big airs and it's unlikely you'll ever need that ambulance. Beaches are definitely a good bet, especially if they have soft sand, as this affords a softer landing. Even so the landings can be heavy. If you do feel that it's all getting a bit too big or you pick up one of those second surges from a gust of wind the best advice is not to let go, hang on to your wrist straps and wait for the kites to bring you down again. The only circumstances in which this does not apply are when the kites are dragging or flying you towards a fixed obstacle such as a post, pier, wall, rock or tree. Take a kite or two off your stack and try again or wait for the wind to drop a little.

▸ *A jumper with a Super 10*

How to jump

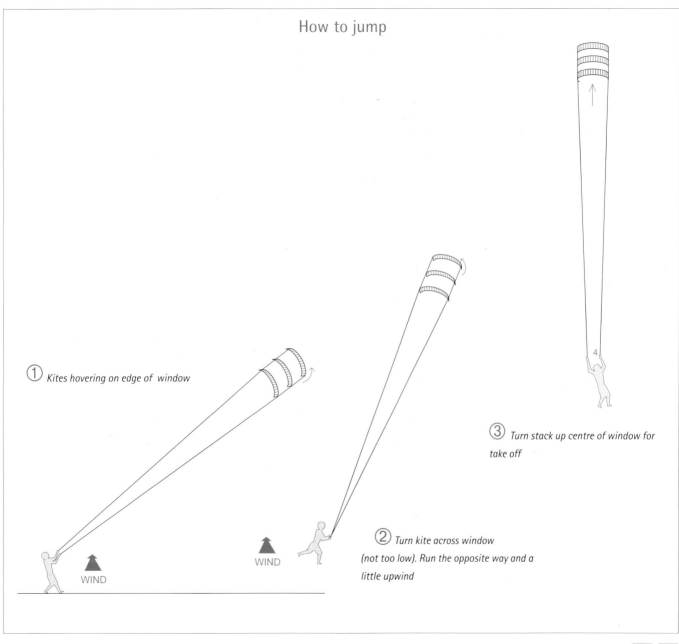

① Kites hovering on edge of window

② Turn kite across window (not too low). Run the opposite way and a little upwind

③ Turn stack up centre of window for take off

WIND

WIND

Four-line
Power Kites

"Soft four-line kites took recreational power kiting to a new level. Now you could use kites as a traction tool to propel the flyer on buggies, kiteboards, mountainboards and anything else that moves!"

Jeremy Pilkington
Sales and Marketing Manager, Flexifoil International

The four-line concept

AS THE FACE OF power kiting has changed and all manner of extra traction possibilities have been opened up by harnessing kite power to include buggies, landboards and of course kiteboarding boards, so the performance requirements for power and traction kites have changed too. The easy-to-use standard Flexifoil kite (or stack), though good enough to get you going for, say, buggying, wasn't specifically designed for the job and so it was no surprise that the company decided to put a clean sheet of paper on the drawingboard when the time came to deal with the new traction challenges. Not least of the issues being re-launch, not at all easy with a stack. Responding to an entirely different set of demands, Flexifoil made a giant evolutionary leap to start developing soft, frameless (no spars or stiffeners) airfoil traction kites, designed to meet the varied needs and usage options in the new power kiting disciplines.

That removal of any frame rod was in itself a radical enough departure for the company, bearing in mind that up to that point it had only ever produced the Flexifoil wings and a range of framed delta wing sport kites. There were already some soft two-line power kites available, notably the Peel, designed by fellow traction pioneer New Zealander, Peter Lynn. These were generally slower moving than Flexifoils but could be made in big enough sizes to deliver the necessary 'grunt' for buggying and the curious buggy-boat that Lynn was also manufacturing at the time, without

the need for stacking. It was clear too from parapente and parachute design that this type of wing could deliver big power. But there was to be another element to the change in format, one that has ultimately done much to facilitate the vast and rapid expansion of appeal in traction kiting.

During the late 1980s, the American kite manufacturer, Revolution, successfully developed their synonymous and truly revolutionary carbon fibre-framed, four-line sport kite, the Revolution #1. Instead of two control lines the new kite had four: two each attached to left and right sides of the kite sail, one at the top and one at the bottom. Special control handles were made with two attachment points on each, one handle controlling each side of the kite. Whereas a two-line kite has its angle of attack (the angle of the sail against the wind) fixed to move the kite forwards all the time, with the new concept it was possible to engage forward movement by applying pressure to the top lines, then apply pressure to the bottom ones, thereby altering the angle of attack so that backwards became forwards, slow the kite, stop it and move it in reverse... In fact, four lines technically gives 360-degree manoeuvrability. This was a curious combination of the kite's ultra-precise flexibility and its ability to stand still that caught the eye. Traction kite designers quickly saw the possibilities and adapted the principle to soft traction foils. It was an enormous success and marked the point at which the numbers of people getting into power kites reached critical mass and the whole market became self-promoting and sustaining.

◄ Bullet 3.5m

▲ Blade III 4m

Lacking a frame, completely soft ram air kites need a multiple suspension point bridle system to hold their shape. Although this is more complex to design and not self-adjusting in flight, what it does mean is that the flyer can control the angle of attack of the kite more using the control handles and so create and use a different kind of lift. The four control lines make that control very sensitive and accurate.

As it applies to power kites, even in the four-line scenario most of the work in terms of load bearing and steering control is effected with the front lines (this is not the case if flying from a control bar or flying an inflatable water kite such as the Storm where the steering is mostly done by the rear lines). The rear lines are there most of the time to help keep the kite in the right shape and for 'braking' it to reduce power. They are much less used for actually going backwards, other than for relaunching from the otherwise impossible face down position. For this reason, generally speaking the front lines are stronger than the rear ones. The control handles are each in the form of a short bar, slightly curved near the top. Top and bottom on left and right sides of the kite connect to the corresponding top and bottom of each handle. There is a risk of attaching your flying lines upside down and nowadays line sets are sold with colour coded sleeved loops so you can tell at a glance which is which. Flying and steering the kite is achieved in very much the same way as before, pulling with left and right hands but keeping pres-

▶ *Four-line control handles wih safety leash*

sure on all four lines to keep the kite in shape. To brake the kite you gradually apply more pressure with the rear lines until the kite slows down to a complete stop and will eventually slowly start moving backwards.

The size and efficiency of these traction kites explains the increasing use of body harnesses, like those used by windsurfers, by serious power kiters. A loop of heavy line connecting the handles is hooked into the harness which enables you to carry most of the pull on your legs and body, relieving pressure on your arms (kiteboarder control bars have purpose-made harness loops). Steering happens as normal with the loop of line sliding through your harness hook or pulley. You shouldn't consider using a harness until you have fully mastered flying your kite ordinarily. It doesn't take long to adapt to flying with four lines but you certainly should spend some time, as ever, fully familiarising yourself with the flying controls of a smaller kite before you get radically powered up.

There's been a long-standing mis-perception of kiting as an activity whose potential is limited by the flying line spaghetti scenario. The idea of four control lines can be quite intimidating in theory but in practice everything is geared towards simplicity. No one wants to waste their time untangling big line messes and nowadays all aspects of power kiting are geared to delivering maximum fun with minimum fuss. Kiting has sorted out its spaghetti issues and you need not worry. You shouldn't have problems if you are organised about how you handle your flying lines. In any event they are a

critical element of the whole kit and need to be respected as much as the kite itself. Always allow time at the end of your session to pack up in an orderly way and always immobilise your kite properly when not in use. Bad winding and a kite that blows away down the field are two common causes of fouled lines.

One major difference with soft aerofoils is that they are very difficult (to the point of virtually impossible) to stack, requiring a different approach to the issue of having more or less power on the end of your control lines. An early idea from one UK manufacturer was a kite wing with extra sections that could be quickly zip fastened on or taken off. But the idea that got the majority vote was to have a range of kites in different sizes that would enable flying in a wide

range of winds. A similar principle is used in sailing boats and windsurfers who use their smallest sails in the biggest winds and vice versa.

In most other respects four-line kites are no different, with the same wind window and other physical limits as their two line predecessors. Some, such as the Blade, can be adapted for flying on a two-line set up. Just because they're soft don't kid yourself that they cannot damage or be damaged. With no other visible means of support (such as a spar or frame) they are more susceptible and sensitive to nicks and tears in the fabric. Overstretching can also be a problem, especially if a kite is flown above its recommended wind range for lengthy periods, not uncommon when a serious buggier or kiteboarder is heavily powered up going for maximum

speed or lift. And a heavy, vent down, fully inflated and powered up landing can easily burst a panel or worse, one of the internal ribs that are critical to the airflow and pressure within the sail. Likewise, with so much power in play, slamming the kite into a bystander could cause them serious injury. Remember, safety is the responsibility of the flyer.

Since the development of soft, aerofoil or 'ram air' power kite wings there's been a quantum leap in the number of power kite manufacturers who've come into the market to satisfy the increasing demand. Flexifoil have always argued that competition is good for the market, stimulating technical advances and product design, all of which can only benefit the consumer. That's certainly true in this increasingly specialised market where the last ten years have been the most productive for Flexifoil and the whole industry. Flexifoil themselves currently have two complete ranges of four-line aerofoil and ram air kite wings, each designed to meet specific needs in the diverse and rapidly evolving demands of modern traction kiting. Two others have recently been deleted from the Flexifoil range as their usefulness has been outstripped by performance requirement.

Quad-line power kites: Blade III and Bullet

Soft kites have no rods or frame to stiffen them; they inflate with wind pressure through a series of vents at the front and are held in shape by a complex bridle structure with multiple suspension points as described earlier. The extra controllability of the four-line set up has made it possible for many more people to enjoy the kite buggy experience with far greater ease, allowing themselves to be pulled along and concentrating more on steering the buggy or landboard,

◀ *Four-line handles – the brake position*

▲ *The harness*

less on piloting these super stable four-line kites. Not surprisingly four-line kites have quickly replaced the generally faster moving two-line foils that had been the option previously. The first big Flexifoil soft kite success, the Skytiger, was designed and developed in 1995 by Jones' original Flexifoil partner, Ray Merry, and his new Cobra Kites venture in America. Because of their long-standing relationship it was only natural that Flexifoil would manufacture and distribute the kite in Europe. The Skytiger has now been superseded by the hugely versatile and successful Blade and more recently the Bullet, but its place in traction kiting history is assured.

The Bullet

"The Bullet is easy for beginners, the perfect training centre kite, while still having the performance to interest more advanced flyers. It's fast, has little or no drag and is designed for traction (lateral) force and stability."

Mike Shaw, Flexifoil UK Sales Manager

The Bullet is the most recent addition to the Flexifoil ram air range, making its debut in 2003. It was designed by Henry Rebbeck and Andrew Jones as Flexifoil's new medium performance land foil. It's an ultra-stable aerofoil, medium aspect ratio kite, semi-eliptical in shape to minimise drag and increase its power-to-size ratio. Like the basic Flexifoil kite it has a gauze-covered leading edge vent running the whole span of the kite to

help 'inflate' the kite quickly for launch or relaunch. There's a multiple bridle suspension line structure, to keep the kite in shape, made from tough-sleeved Dyneema. The Bullet is powerful but still easy to handle. It's available in four sizes, from 1.5 to 4.5 square metres, the two smaller sizes being good beginner traction kites but the larger sizes requiring at least intermediate skill level because, despite their super stable handling, they develop serious amounts of grunt! The Bullet is fantastically versatile, a great all-rounder and suitable for all land-based power kite activities, such as they exist today, recreational flying, buggying, landboarding and snowkiting. What it is not is a 'water' kite. That's to say you should not, under any circumstances, try to use the Bullet on the water. There are other toys in

the Flexifoil cupboard much better suited to that kind of thing.

The latest twist in the power kite tale has taken them onto the water with the successful invention and popularising of kiteboarding. Like windsurfing, but using a kite for power instead of a fixed mast and sail, kiteboarding has brought its particular set of requirements to bear on the creative forces behind modern kite design. Like many of the pioneering kiteboard manufacturers, Flexifoil's first solution to the kite for water board use was already established as the Formula One model in their ram air foil range when kiteboarding first started – the Blade.

▲ *The Bullet*

▶ *Buggying with the Bullet in the Nevada Desert*

The Blade

The Blade, another Andrew Jones original design, is now in its third generation of development as a frameless aerofoil kite with a multiple bridle and a high aspect ratio. Recognising they had a great basic design, Blades were the kites used by Flexifoil's three-man team on their successful first ever channel crossing by kiteboard in 1999

Flexifoil have listened to what their customers have said about the first two Blade generations, positive and negative. The resulting refinements and improvements which Luke Rebbeck has included on the Blade III reflect that and make it one of the most sophisticated and best performing ram air kites on the market. It has an ellipsoidal outline with rounded wing tips, a well-proven wing form giving a solid structure and good aerodynamic properties across the whole span. It's a kite for intermediate to expert level flyers that develops phenomenal pull and lift to help keep the kiteboard rider well up on the water despite the fact that it's not a water relaunchable kite. In fact the

◀ *Kiteboarding with the Blade III*

▶ *Blade Mark 1 getting big air near Dover*

Blade was originally developed and is excellent for land use too, and is a popular choice for buggy drivers and landboarders etc. It's available in six different sizes reflecting the extremes and range of conditions you need to understand when you start to play with these very serious 'toys'. On the Blade III by varying the aspect ratios of the different sizes the Flexifoil design team have ensured that they all handle similarly making it simple to switch kite because of a wind change. Likewise the wing tips have a thinner aerofoil section, improving the kite's turn speed, plus wing tip vents to facilitate emptying of sand, water and snow from inside the kite. .

A quick look at the photos on pages 56-60 will show you what the kites look like and how much they differ from their predecessors. You can use them both equally well out of a buggy or off the water, flying them for fun or as part of your education. Of course it's a good idea to totally familiarise yourself with every new kite wing you fly and learning the kites first is the only way to approach the added risks of buggies and boards, so inevitably you're going to end up flying the kite simply as a kite at some point. You'll find that you'll be able to skid and jump as before, much more in fact as now the chances are you'll be flying bigger wings to suit your changing traction habits and your ever-increasing mastery of the kites and their power. But a vast range of other traction possibilities awaits you once you're into four-line foils.

Both the Blade and Bullet can be flown using a choice of either control bar or independent handles. Different activities may be better suited to different systems so make sure you discuss thoroughly with your dealer before purchasing and make sure they actually give you the correct one.

In the case of the Blade, an extra bonus is that the control bar can be used with either the four-line set up, or with a two-line conversion kit set up you can fit to the kite. Some board riders (kiteboarder Chris Calthrop included) prefer the simplicity of two-line flying, the combination of stability and speed of the kite ideally suited to their style of riding. Whereas the Bullet is always a four line kite no matter which control system you choose.

The switch back to control bars brings things neatly full circle; Flexifoil kites originally came with just such a control bar although in those days it was a simple bar made of wood, not the contoured, carbon composite, technical bars used today. Using a control bar is enormously different from independent handles.

If you're used to flying your Blade on handles, make sure you fully familiarise yourself with the differences in handling your kite before you try any serious traction action if you do decide to switch to a control bar.

Setting up and packing up procedures

When you buy a Blade or Bullet it will come in a funky carry bag. To give it its full technical description, it's a padded, customised backpack bag with moisture vent and control gear storage (it holds your handles and bar as well as the kite). Inside the bag you should find – the kite – neatly folded, a pair of four-line control handles or a control bar with colour-coded flying lines, an instruction manual, a product registration card and a one month free repair card. If any of these items is missing contact your dealer or Flexifoil International immediately. You are well advised to go home and take the kite out in the calm comfort of your living room to have a good look at it there before you take the often sizeable sail out to a windy flying field, where it can all too easily turn into a flapping monster, while you are holding the instruction book in your teeth. You will also need to make sure you have appropriate strength flying lines for your new kite. Make sure you ask your dealer for the right lines for your kite. There's a table on page 180 showing line strengths which are for average use; for serious traction activities or strong winds you may need to upgrade these in which case contact your dealer.

Follow the manufacturer's instructions for setting up and packing up and you won't have any difficulties. In the unlikely event that you do have a problem, take the kite back to your local dealer for advice or contact Flexifoil direct; their details are given at the end of the book. Try to remember how the kite was packed when you first unfold it and try always to repack it the same way. See also the care and maintenance of your equipment section of the book for other recommended storage and other packing tips. Your instruction manual also covers setting

▲ *The correct take-off position*

up your flying lines and attaching your control handles or control bar. You will need to be familiar with the lark's head knot to correctly attach your flying lines so if you skipped that bit of the earlier section covering basic Flexifoil kites it's time to go back and check it out now.

Whether you fly them using handles or control bar, both the Blade and Bullet come fitted with a safety leash which you should use at all times. The system is quite straightforward to use: a simple cord comes from the handles or bar, attaching to your wrist by a velcro strap. The leash is attached to the brake or rear lines (these do exist on the Blade two-line set up in order to operate the safety system although they can't actually be used to steer the kite). Using handles you

will have one safety leash for each handle / wrist. Using a control bar there is just one leash running through an eyelet on the control bar centre; it's up to you which wrist you attach it to. The safety leash can be actioned any time you feel that the situation you're in or getting into is too much for you to deal with the classic being over-powered and going too fast for comfort. If all other attempts to control the kite fail you simply let go of the handles or bar. The leash pulls on the brake lines of your kite but the front lines are released, spilling all air virtually instantaneously from the kite, de-powering it almost completely and bringing it harmlessly back down to land or water. It's easy then to recover the controls and relaunch your kite. A few practice goes will soon have it under control and will prepare you for when you need to use it for real. The safety leash is there for your and other site users' safety: make sure you use it always.

So, having fastened your velcro straps to set the safety leash, make sure your open space is still free of other people and obstacles and check that the wind hasn't changed direction; it can be very shifty at times, specially inland. It's recommended that you make your first few flights in light to moderate wind until you get used to how the kite handles and pulls. If it's all looking good at this point you're ready to fly:

How to launch, fly and land using independent handles

Launching the kite

Under normal circumstances you should be able to solo launch.

- pick up the handles, remembering to put your ground stake in one pocket as you'll need it later to immobilise the kite and lines again.
- take one handle in each hand holding them firmly by the foam cushioned section at the top, curve away from you and the bottom of the handles further towards the kite than the top. The front flying line leaders should come out from between your index and second fingers and your thumbs should be on top of the

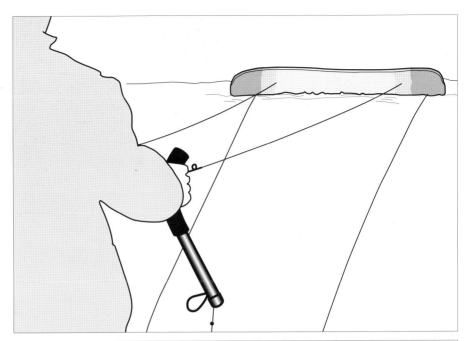

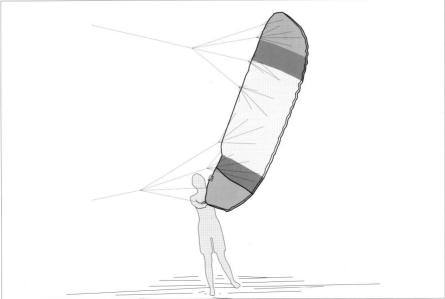

▸ *Top: Solo launch*
▸ *Bottom: Assisted launch*

top of the handle, joystick style. This is the 'neutral' position for normal flight.

- make a last-minute check that your lines are connected correctly, left to left and right to right, top to top etc., and untwisted. The wind should be on your back with you and the kite in centre window. The kite should still be on its back and the trailing edge weighted down.
- pull back gently and steadily with both handles keeping equal pressure on all four lines. The front or leading edge of the kite will lift up and the kite begin to inflate with wind pressure. As it inflates the kite will stand up on its trailing edge ready to take off. You can hold it at this point by pushing forward slightly with both thumbs until you're absolutely ready for flying.
- pull sharply on all four lines to fully inflate the kite and it will start to lift off. You may need to take a few steps back to get it moving depending on the wind conditions. The kite will fly straight up the wind window as long as you pull evenly on all four lines, through the power zone, to come to a rest with minimum power in the 'park' position at the top centre or zenith of the window. Be ready to deal with the pull as the kite hits the power zone, leaning back with your shoulders and moving forwards a little on the ground.

Let's take a quick look at the other solo launch method and assisted launching. In strong winds it's inadvisable to launch in centre window as the kite will hit the strongest power zone of the window immediately after launch and can be very dangerous for you and other people.

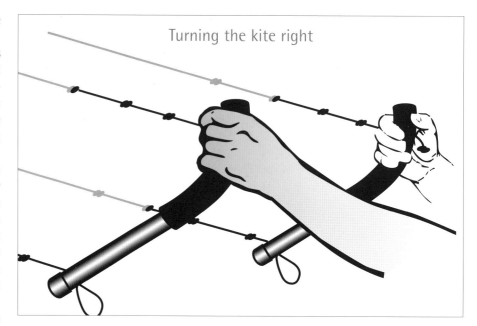

Turning the kite right

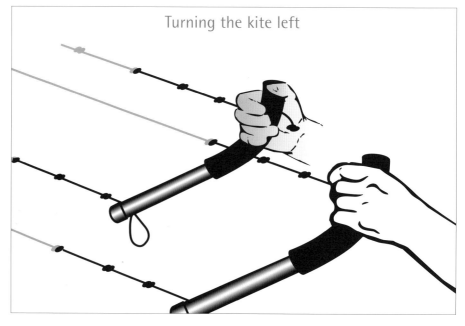

Turning the kite left

- you need to set the kite up close to the edge of the wind window in relation to where you stand at window centre. Lay the kite on its back but this time lengthways downwind so that the wind blows across the kite from tip to tip, leading-edge vents facing towards the edge of the window. Weight down the upwind tip with sand, leaving the downwind tip free.
- pick up your handles and pull gently on the downwind end of the kite (the tip furthest away) which will lift the tip and leading edge enough to allow the kite to inflate.
- keep pulling steadily with the downwind handle and the kite will launch and fly itself towards the edge of the wind window.

- keep pulling slightly on the downwind handle and steer the kite carefully up the edge of the wind window to the zenith where you can neutralise your steering and get ready for action.

If using an assisted launch make sure your helper understands what to do:

- first of all they should stand towards the edge of the window, behind the kite, holding it up so that the leading edge is facing the wind, pointing towards the edge of the wind window.
- once the kite is inflated and you're ready, call to the helper to release the kite, simply letting it go rather than trying to throw the kite up which will actually prevent a smooth take off.
- as they release, you fly the kite out of their hands pulling slightly on the upper tip to steer the kite up, the edge of the wind window to the zenith.

Flying and steering the kite
You can hold the kite at the zenith for as long as you like but as soon as you're ready you should start with some basic turns. To begin with, keep the kite high in the wind window and make gentle control movements. This will keep it out of the extreme pull of the power zone while you get used to

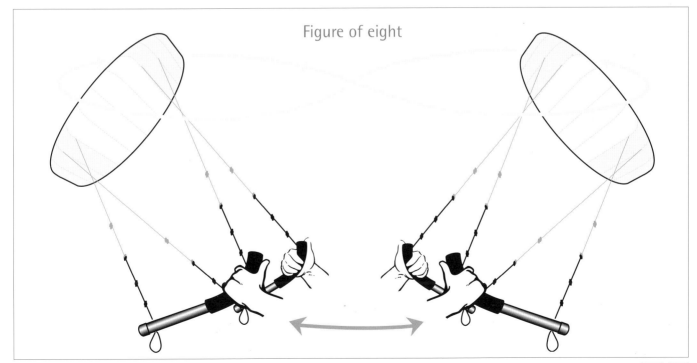

Figure of eight

the handling. The basic turn manoeuvre is similar to a two line kite.

- when the kite is climbing up the middle of the wind window and is nearing the zenith, pull back on the right handle keeping tension on both lines. The kite turns to the right and starts making a wide, full loop in that direction.
- keep pulling on the right handle until the kite has flown a complete circle and is climbing up the wind window again, pointing straight up.
- bring your handles back to the neutral position and the kite flies straight up.
- now pull on the left handle to execute a left loop and untwist your flying lines.

You will find that as much as you pull with one handle you push with the other because of the angle of your body and this in fact makes a good, smooth turn. A pull with one hand 'stalls' one side of the kite and the other speeds up around it. Pushing with the opposite one makes a similar but smoother turn by keeping the whole kite moving. You can also start to make different and even better turns by using the extra control possibilities of the two extra lines:

- as you begin a loop, whichever handle is being pulled should be pivoted so that the rear line is pulled as well as the top. Push your thumb away from you and point the top of the handle more towards the kite. The kite will turn faster, even spin on its axis, before resuming full power.
- as the kite comes round full circle bring the

▲ *The three stages of landing*

handles back to the neutral position to resume normal flying.

As your flying become more confident you can experiment with more power. Flying alternate left and right loops in a kind of flat figure of eight in the centre of the wind window will give the best and most consistent pull as a fixed flyer (as opposed to one moving on a board or buggy) and stop the lines twisting too much.

Four-line control with handles means having the ability to stop and reverse the kite, even de-power it if needed. It requires a lot of wrist action and brings the rear lines fully into play. You stop the kite in mid air by changing the aerodynamics:

- with the kite flying up the middle of the window, leading edge pointing straight up, rotate both handles by pointing your thumbs forward until the kite 'brakes'.
- keep pulling on the rear lines and the kite slows to a stop and starts to reverse.
- to resume normal flying, rotate the handles back to the neutral position by bringing your thumbs towards you again and pull on the front lines.

With experience you'll be able to control the rear lines much better. Fine adjustments of your braking and playing the handles a little will enable you to position and hold the kite just where you want it almost anywhere in the window.

Reverse launching and landing

▶ *Reverse landing from the edge of the window in strong winds*

▶ *Reverse landing from the centre of the window*

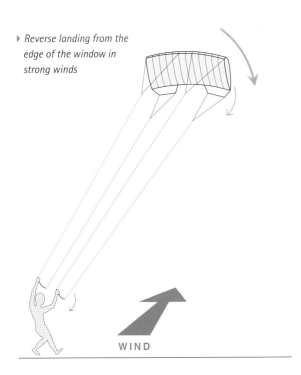

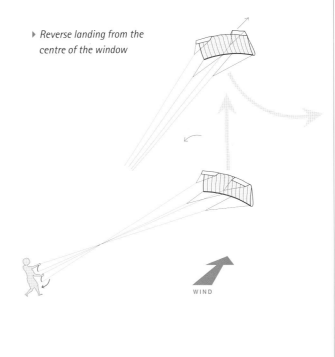

▶ *Reverse launching your kite*

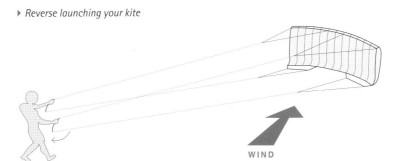

Landing the kite

Landing is an extended version of stopping and reversing the kite. Technically speaking it can be done anywhere in the wind window as long as the leading edge is pointing up. In practice you may find that it's easier to begin with trying it nearer to the edge of the wind window where there's less power in the sail. Be careful, though; too close to the edge could make the kite unstable and require some juggling to keep it steady:

- with the kite pointing straight up, as close to the ground as you can and your handles in the neutral position, apply almost full brakes by rotating both wrists so the top of the handles are pointing at the kite. You should be flying on virtually the brake lines only. The kite slows and stops very quickly, de-powering it.
- keep the rear lines on full. The kite will descend backwards to the ground and settle on its trailing edge. Don't try to go too fast backwards or it may 'flip out', bottom towards you. You may well need to play the handles quite a lot coming down the last few metres to keep the kite steady.

It will take a bit of practice to get right but once you've landed it's up to you whether you want to relaunch or stop flying. Relaunch as you launched first time. To immobilise the kite, peg the handles to the ground by the loops at the bottom, keeping tension on the rear lines as you do so. Then go and weight the kite down.

▶ *Blade's two-line crossover conversion kit*

Relaunching and recovering the kite

Another advantage of four-line flying is that you can relaunch from almost any position. Generally you'll find that the kite is either on its trailing edge, in which case relaunch is obvious, or its leading edge (going forwards into the ground), making re-launch a little less obvious. But if you can reverse the kite in the sky it logically follows that you can reverse it off the ground too. This is what's known as reverse launching:

- with the kite on the ground, fully inflated and standing on its leading edge, pull backwards (it may need you to walk backwards a few steps too) with the rear lines only. The kite should begin to rise backwards of the ground. You will often need to 'play' the handles to keep it going steadily.
- keep pulling back on the rear lines and, as the kite rises, push one of the rear lines forward by pivoting the handle and the kite will pivot. It's easier to turn the kite up and away from window centre rather than down towards it as the kite will tend to accelerate towards centre window and into the ground.
- when it's pointing straight up the window you can fly away or try another landing if that's what you were doing.

If that doesn't work there's another thing you can try. It involves turning the kite onto its trailing edge so the leading edge is pointing straight up, then you can relaunch in the usual way. This is normally easiest if you try to roll it over towards the window centre. If the kite is directly downwind of you, walk a

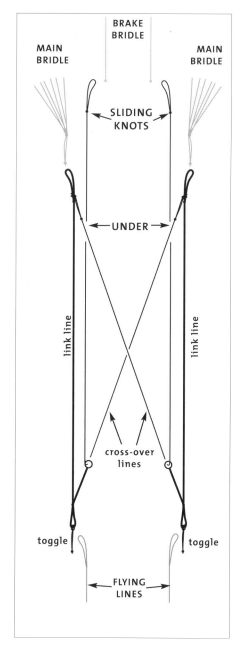

few paces to one side to create a new centre window which will automatically create a new position for the kite, closer to the edge of the window:

- pull back on one handle only, the one connected to the side of the kite furthest from window centre, the bottom of the handle more than the top. The tip of the kite will lift up and rise until the kite is standing vertically, its leading edge pointing out of the wind window.
- at this point you can start bringing the handle you pulled slowly back to the neutral position, still with more pressure on the bottom line. The kite should continue to roll down to a horizontal position, its leading edge pointing up.
- as the kite reaches the correct position use your rear lines to keep it still on the ground while you get ready to launch in the normal way.

Troubleshooting

Nothing should go wrong but if for any reason the kite doesn't perform there are a few things you can check:

- the bridles are not twisted.
- the flying lines are correctly attached, heaviest lines on the front, left lines to left handle
- you've got the handles in the correct hands.
- that one or all the lines haven't stretched. In fact, stretching can occur during your first few sessions, until the lines are fully flown in. Check your lines regularly to make sure they are still all the same length. What to do about this is explained in the 'Care of

your kit' in chapter 7.

- if the kite is sluggish on take off and slow through the sky the chances are that your brake lines are too short or the main lines are too long.
- if the kite is unresponsive to steering and difficult to reverse check whether either the brake lines are too long or the main lines too short.
- in either of the above scenarios you can make an adjustment at the handles, shortening or lengthening as appropriate, using the leader line knots.
- if the tips or trailing edge are flapping there may be sand in the kite. Land and empty the sand out through the vents at the front.

If the kite still won't fly, contact your dealer or Flexifoil International direct. Expect to learn very quickly. Talk to other, more experienced flyers if you can. Their advice can save you an awful lot of learning-from-your-mistakes time. After a few sessions you'll be a fully competent power kite flyer and ready for some serious action.

Flying the kites on a control bar

There's a growing number of kiteboarders, both water and snow varieties, who prefer the sophistication of top range kites like the Blade with the simplicity of control bar flying. It's true that flying a kite on a control bar is in a sense simpler but you sacrifice some control finesse with that. And a bar makes a much better 'trapeze' for aerial gymnastics. You could choose to fly with a two-line set up as described. On the other hand there are those kiteboarders who

prefer the four-line configuration on a control bar because it reduces kite speed but increases manoeuvrability and controllability. Flying four line on a control bar doesn't, however, give you the full mobility of independent handles so you won't have the same control for reverse landing, for example.

There's also a significant number of power kiters who prefer to fly using a control bar because of the additional safety options and because it's better suited to the activity they want to do. For instance, land and kiteboarding are generally easier using a control bar whereas buggying simply wouldn't be an option because, with your body movement much more limited (sitting down) you couldn't get enough independent movement of your hands.

Every Blade kite can be flown on a Blade control bar fitted with either the four-line set up or a two-line conversion crossover kit to transform it from a four to a two-line kite. The main effect of fitting the crossover kit is to help speed up the turn rate of the kite although the performance of the Blade 3 on four lines is such that there is little difference in air and turn speed now. Crossover kits can be purchased separately and you'll also need to buy yourself the control bar for actually flying the kite, preferably a Flexifoil model but you could use another make. Flexifoil recommend bars between 60 and 65 cm long although it's down to your own preference in the end. A general rule of thumb for beginners is to use a longer bar with a bigger kite and vice versa. Longer bars tend to make the kites more (possibly over) reactive. Follow the step by step instructions for fitting the cross over kit that are included in your Blade II instruction manual. If in doubt, consult your local dealer or Flexifoil International.

Likewise every Bullet kite can be flown on a Bullet control bar, the difference being that the Bullet is only designed for four-line flying. The bar for the smallest size, the 1.5 m^2, is different from the bar for the others; which are respectively 60 and 65cm long. Generally speaking you will lose some of the fine manoeuvrability of handles when you switch to using a control bar but the price is worth paying if it actually allows you to do what you want to do more easily. You don't need the same degree of manoeuvrability and you don't get it.

All the control bars have a built in safety system. This comprises a wrist leash attached to the rear (brake) lines sliding through an eyelet or slot in the centre of the control bar. In the event of getting into unrecoverable difficulty you can simply let go of the control bar. It will slide up as far as a stop on the rear lines keeping those taut, allowing front lines to extend and the kite sail to de-power itself, drifting harmlessly back to the ground and allowing you to recover it safely and with no bother.

Launching the kite

Whichever kite you're flying, you're now ready to attach the lines or control bar as previously described. Make sure the lines are untwisted and get your body in position ready to launch. You can solo launch in

▸ *Ready for the launch*

Solo launching

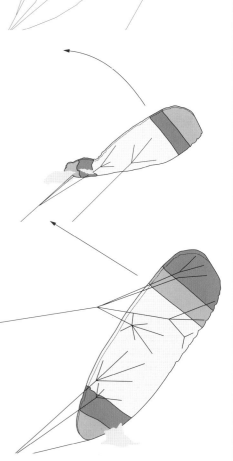

▸ *Lay the kite out on the ground (or have your helper hold the kite up to the wind) lengthways downwind with the leading edge facing the edge of the window. Weight the upwind tip down with sand leaving the downwind tip free.*

▸ *Pull on the downwind (furthest away) tip with your control bar, pulling slowly and steadily. The free tip of the kite will begin to rise and the kite will start inflating as wind enters through the vents.*

▸ *Keep pulling on the furthest tip (you may need to take a couple of steps back) and when the kite is fully inflated it will lift off and turn itself to face upwind; call to your helper to let go in the recommended manner. Steer the kite carefully up the edge of the window to the zenith by pulling gently on the upper tip of the kite with the control bar. Then bring the bar to a 'neutral' position to 'park' the kite there.*

lighter winds but in a strong wind you must launch with a helper. In any event, you have less control over the kite if you're trying the two-line kit and you will need to set up nearer the edge of the window.

Steering

As before, keep the kite high in the window while you get used to how it handles. Turning is done by pulling one side of the bar towards you and pushing the other away, pivoting it around the centre. Pull right to go right, pull left to go left. It will feel different from how the kite flies on handles so take some time to accustom yourself to its handling before you hit full power. But it's still the same kite and will perform in the same way as regards how and where in the wind window it pulls. Practice some figure of eight manoeuvres so you fly alternate left and right loops, making sure you can do it well to both sides.

Now that you're flying on a control bar you will not be able to slow the kite down, stop or reverse, of course, so if at any stage you need to lose some power you will need to fly the kite out to the edge of the wind window, either at one side or at the zenith.

Landing

Without the ability to reverse land, this too will be done differently. You can self-land in light to moderate winds using the same technique as landing a basic Flexifoil kite.

- with the kite flying up the centre of the wind window pull on one side of the control bar to execute a loop.

- when the kite has made half of its loop and is pointing towards the other side of the wind window, bring the control bar to neutral and fly a (low) horizontal pass, taking the kite out to the side of the wind window it's facing.
- keep flying it in that direction until it loses power, steering it towards the ground. It will fall to the ground when it is out of the window.
- quickly go and retrieve your kite, weighting it down with sand or whatever comes to hand, not sharp or pointed objects, otherwise it could easily blow away. If you are carrying a ground stake so much the better,;put the stake firmly in the ground then hook the harness loop (if you've got a Blade bar) or the rear lines at the safety stop over the stake. This will apply the brake lines, immobilising the kite but you should still go and weight the kite down for maximum safety..
- or simply steer the kite from the zenith down the edge of the wind window (by pulling back slightly on one side of the control bar) until the kite comes to ground.

Safety note: If landing in a strong wind you will need a helper to grab the kite and immobilise it for you. Follow the steps as described below.

- fly the kite out to one side of the wind window.
- steer the kite down near to the ground.
- your helper should approach the kite from downwind, behind it, well clear of the lines. Keep the kite as still as possible, close to the

ground, until they are able to grab one tip and then pull the kite down.
- as soon as your helper has grabbed the kite you should release the tension on the flying lines by taking a couple of steps forward towards the kite. Once the helper has immobilised the kite by weighting it down with sand or whatever comes to hand you can stake down the control bar using the loop at the rear or rear line stop if you wish.

Landing the kite on two lines

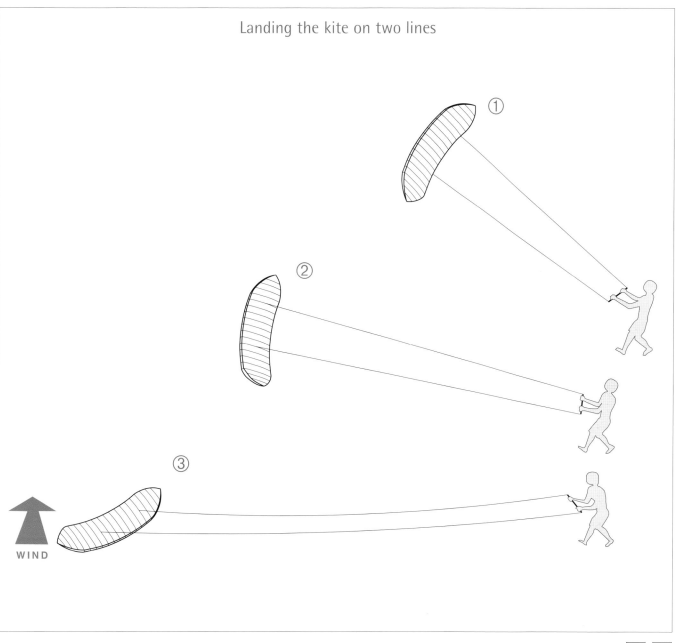

Buggying

"Moving with the wind the first time you bomb down the beach is just awesome. Then you suddenly think 'how do I stop?!' but it helps amazingly for making the transition on to a kiteboard."

Andreya Wharry
Professional kiteboarder and power kite instructor

What is kite buggying?

The idea is very simple. Fly a large single kite or stack of smaller ones, sufficient to generate enough power to pull yourself along. Sit in your vehicle and manipulate them in such a way as to pull you and it along.

A modern power kite and kite buggy are sophisticated adrenaline sport tools, specifically designed for the job, generating speeds up to 50mph, the result of more than 15 years of intensive commercial research and development. When you sit down in a kite buggy with the control handles in your hands you know you're in for a thrill and it's an immense buzz, travelling low down, open to the elements. Even your first 5mph run feels like 50. A bang up-to-date toy in all respects, but moving around by kite power is by no means a new idea.

It's a much repeated story but one worth telling again. The idea of using kite power on a wheeled vehicle is anything but new. During the late 18th century, in the south west of England around Bristol, George Pocock was experimenting with kite traction using large kites attached to a carriage.

About 200 years later, despite Merry and Jones' best early efforts at getting mobile, long-standing traction addict colleague, New Zealander Peter Lynn, is widely credited with being the inventor of a successful modern kite vehicle. This time it's a single seat buggy version, three-wheeled with the driver sitting low to the ground over the rear axle, flying kites with his hands and steering the single front wheel with his feet. And this time the kite is a modern, two-lined, soft aerofoil kite, in Lynn's case called a Peel, on account of its pointed, eliptical shape making it resemble a slice of orange peel.

The buggy frame is stainless steel and it uses high quality bearings. Its simple 'basket' style webbing seat means that it's very easy to be pulled out of the buggy, leading to many spectacular wipe outs. The kites are not specifically designed for the job, they just happen to be what's available.

Kite power existed and people were hunting around for something to do with it. The whole package was far from perfect but, nevertheless, kite buggying was born and has not in essence changed format since, despite the countless buggies and traction kites there are on the market today.

The first Lynn buggies appeared in the mid to late 1980s but manufacturing costs were so high they were very expensive, as were many of the kites to power them, putting them out of the reach of the average kite flying Joe. Although the idea of buggying was sold as something you could do anywhere you could find a large, flat area, the reality was that clearly a buggy was most at home on big hard sandy beaches or mud and salt flats, where the wind is smooth and you can roll for literally miles.

The buggy scene grew painfully slowly for a while, but grow it steadily did. Then, in 1992 the first soft four-line ram air kites appeared and other kite and buggy manufacturers were starting to get involved as the sales volumes slowly increased and prices therefore dropped. Flexifoil commissioned its

◀ Flexifoil's production buggy

▶ An original Peter Lynn buggy

▲ Original and sports buggies

own earliest commercial buggy designs from Peter Lynn in 1994, then launched its Skytiger series in 1995 and suddenly buggying took off big time.

Within a couple of years a full national and international competition race circuit, club and society network had grown up as all of a sudden kite buggying began to appeal to adrenaline sports people from beyond the kite scene. The surge of interest in the mid 1990s brought in new and different ideas and equipment developed fast. Needless to say, Flexifoil has been at the forefront of the whole traction scene, supporting events and organisations, sponsoring drivers (and now kiteboarders). Products have developed at an astonishing rate and kite buggying is a vastly different beast nowadays. Flexifoil alone has two ranges of kites that can be used for buggying, the Blade and Bullet series, and it's now

a highly specialised business.

The latest Flexifoil buggy is an even more robust design by one of the UK's leading and most extreme buggy pilots, Rob Hills, following extensive R&D work and is designed for even more extreme usage, specially jumping with the buggy. There is also a range of extras available for you to customise your buggy for different terrains making it a buggy that's perfect for beginners and pros alike. It features an adjustable downtube on the front fork to cater for most sizes of rider; curved footrests to help keep your feet in position; a hi-grade wide stainless steel, tube frame for strength and stability; a wrap around seat and contoured frame for comfort and back support; stainless steel bolts and specially engineered fittings; a splashguard for muddy fields and dirty beaches.

Buggying's natural beach habitat made it a logical next step to go on the water, too, as has now happened with kiteboarding, but

you can argue that the water version would never have happened without buggying sorting so many issues out beforehand. The surf version has somewhat eclipsed buggying of late, media-wise at least, but that can't hide the fact that more and more people are coming to buggying too as part of the big wave of interest in kite traction tomfoolery.

The rules of the road

Let's say this now because before you go anywhere near a buggy you need to understand a few things. Good buggying means safe and responsible buggying because the danger to yourself and other people is considerable:

- do not attempt to kite buggy until you have fully mastered your kite.
- never attach yourself permanently to the kite. Use extreme caution.

- never use your buggy in conditions that are too extreme for your skill level and equipment.
- never kite buggy if you cannot safely handle the power of your kite; use a smaller kite or wait for lighter wind.
- avoid gusty winds which can be very difficult for inexperienced flyers.
- avoid all other kite contra indications (lightning, power cables, roads, airports etc.).
- always behave in a responsible manner and respect other site users.
- always select a site with a big, clear space all around you, free of people, obstructions and sharp objects.
- always disable your kite and lines when not in use and avoid unsecured kites on the ground.
- never buggy on busy beaches or anywhere you could injure someone.
- always obtain permission to use the site if appropriate.
- respect nature, the site and other users at all times; always clear up your rubbish.
- check all your equipment regularly (kites, buggy, flying lines, harness and other safety gear) before use.
- do not use worn or damaged equipment; repair or replace it immediately.
- always use appropriate safety equipment.
- be aware of your flying lines at all times. These can cause serious injury when under tension from a powered-up kite.
- take out third-party liability insurance that covers buggying.

▶ *Flexifoil buggy in action*

▲ *Trick style: Two wheel riding*

▶ *A big foot buggy*

In short, use your common sense ! There will be plenty of buzz to come without taking unnecessary risks.

Getting started

You'll want the right kind of kite for buggying and what that almost certainly means is:

- four lines so you can 'lock' the kite in the power zone and regulate the power by changing the angle of attack.
- a relatively thin profile to reduce lateral pull.
- a big wind window to make getting back upwind easier.
- mobility around the window to guarantee

continuous access to maximum power.
- good edge handling and performance.
- smooth (as opposed to abrupt) acceleration to reduce the tendency to pull the driver out of the buggy.

And since both the Blade and Bullet fit that bill you've already made one good buggying decision before you start.

It's possible to learn buggying on your own, after all, the people who invented it had to make it up as they went along, but a good idea might be to try one of the Flexifoil approved buggy schools where you can learn the basics and try out different equipment in complete (and insured!) safety before committing your cash.

At this point you will need to have your

own buggy, which may be a Flexifoil model or one of the many others on the market. Follow the manufacturer's instructions for assembling whichever buggy you have. Make sure the wheels are tightly bolted on and the tyres inflated to the correct pressure.

There are three different widths of tyres you can fit to your buggy. The most versatile are the standard wide ones. Wide wheels spread the load over a wide area and prevent the buggy sinking in the sand. Even so, for very soft sand you might one day want to invest in a set of Flexifoil's giant extra wide wheels, which can be fitted onto a standard Flexifoil buggy rear axle. You might also want to change to an extra wide axle, which improves stability, upwind performance and is great for racing. The third option, rarely used generally and not at all by Flexifoil, is narrow wheels, which are good for hard ground or even metalled road type surfaces such as old airfields.

Like all aspects of power kiting you are better advised to start learning in a light to moderate wind, up to 15mph, as the kite will pull less and everything will be happening slower. You'll need to multi-function and there's definitely a bit of brain overload to begin with as you get used to controlling the kite and buggy simultaneously, so slowing everything down a little can really help.

Check the wind direction carefully, especially if you're using a coastal site. The best wind on a beach will be an on-shore, coming onto the beach from the sea. Not only will it be smooth, since the aim will be to 'sail' backwards and forwards across the wind it will allow you to run up and down the length of the beach and keep you out of the water. An off-shore wind will probably be lumpy and drive you out into the water more.

Clearly you're going to need a vastly bigger space than ever before, especially while you're learning and can't fully control what you do. Here's how it should happen and refer to the diagrams on page 80.

① Your buggy should be pointing at 45 degrees to the wind direction, downwind to help you get going. Then:
• once the buggy is moving you will be trying to steer across the wind so as not to lose too much ground forwards. You can run downwind but you're going to have a long and uncomfortable walk back carrying all that equipment with the wind against you. Your first objective is to learn how to buggy across the wind.
• launch your kite and take it to the minimum power position at the zenith while you approach the buggy from the downwind side. This is to avoid you suddenly being pulled forward by a big gust causing you to fall on the buggy.
• keeping the kite at the zenith, straddle the buggy and sit down in it. At this point you still have some resistance from your feet.
• put one foot (upwind) on its foot peg, the other still holding you from being pulled forward.
② You are committed to going towards the side the buggy is pointing so carefully steer the kite down the edge of the window you want to go towards. Never take the kite back to the other side of the window as this will result in you being pulled backwards out of the buggy.
• as you feel the power coming into the kite lift your other foot up onto its foot peg and steer slightly downwind to get the buggy moving.
③ Lock the kite in position at roughly 45 degrees to the ground and keep tension on the flying lines as the buggy gets going to avoid running over your own lines. Try to steer the buggy more across the wind. Remember to watch where you're going as well as the kite. You should be flying on the front lines mostly, just using the rear lines to keep the tension and hold the kite in position. If you're going too fast take the kite further up the wind window, which will reduce power and slow you down.
• keeping moving is easier in reasonably steady wind than light wind. As the kite comes down the edge of the wind window it wants to power you in that direction. You lock your kite at 45 degrees to the ground and try to steer the buggy slightly up and across the wind. In a light wind you will need to work the kite more, flying a continuous figure of eight pattern on the edge of the window. This is easier said than done when you're also steering the buggy, watching for other site users etc.

The tuning of your four-line kite becomes quickly apparent, giving, if correctly set up, the ability to hit the brakes very hard for an instant de-power, even to land the kite if it all gets too much. But, more significantly, it's the

How to get your buggy moving

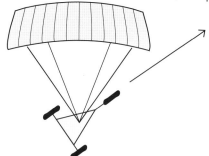

① Buggy pointing at 45 degrees to wind direction. Kite at zenith

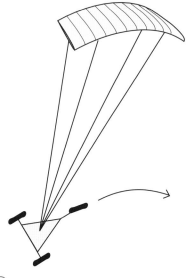

② Kite carefully steered down edge of window. Buggy steered slightly downwind to get moving if needed

③ Kite locked in position. Buggy steered more across wind

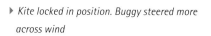

WIND

four line control that allows you to lock the kite in position. And that's why four line kites are so popular, helping you reduce the brain overload and concentrate more on buggying.

Another factor which comes into play once you start moving forwards, across the wind is the phenomenon of 'apparent wind'. Imagine you are sitting in the buggy, pointing at right angles to the wind (wind blowing from one side). The kite is above your head and as you steer it down the window, so you bring it to a hover in front of the buggy and it starts to pull you along. As you speed up, the wind will appear to come more from in front of you, blowing into your face. The combination of the true wind and the wind from your forward motion is the apparent wind.

Buggying at right angles to the true wind, the apparent wind will increase the faster you go, causing the kite to pull harder, increasing your speed even more. Steering slightly upwind gives the optimum apparent wind but be careful not to steer yourself too far upwind and lose power as a result. And not only will apparent wind blow harder, it will come more from in front causing the kite to fly more downwind of you. The result of this could eventually be a big sideways skid or you being pulled out of the buggy sideways. Take the kite higher in the window to lose power and a little speed. And aim for a point just upwind of where you actually want to go to allow for this sideways pull. Kites which move around a lot (for example, two-line kites) will have a more variable apparent wind and less consistent power.

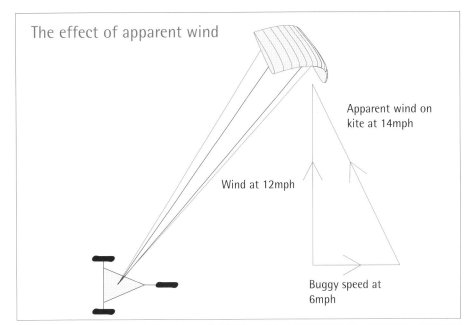

The effect of apparent wind

Apparent wind on kite at 14mph

Wind at 12mph

Buggy speed at 6mph

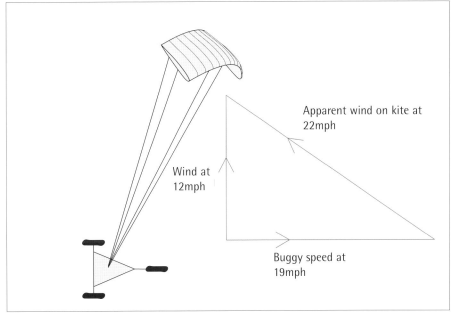

Apparent wind on kite at 22mph

Wind at 12mph

Buggy speed at 19mph

Stopping the buggy

Do not under any circumstances try and stop the buggy by putting your feet down. The chances of catapulting yourself from the buggy or breaking an ankle are very high. There's a perfectly simple way of slowing down and stopping that you should start practising as soon as you start learning how to move:

- whilst driving along across, down or upwind, start steering the kite up the edge of the wind window, pointing straight up. This is done by pulling equally on the two lines attached to the tip which is highest in the window, assuming you have the kite almost vertical on the edge of the window, so you pull back in fact with one handle. At the same time start steering the buggy a little upwind. The kite will begin to lose power and the buggy will slow down.
- stop the kite high up in the centre window pointing upwards (not across the window) and steer the buggy a little more upwind. The more you resist the kite the more you slow down. You will come to a stop with the kite flying just behind you above your head, in the minimum power position.

Don't expect to come to a sudden stop, it will be a gradual slowing down at first. It's all a question of timing and one part in particular of the timing is crucial. With the kite flying behind you there is a big possibility you will be pulled out of the buggy, or along in the buggy, backwards. Take the kite too quickly behind you, too far behind or with too much power and you're in trouble. The only thing then is to try and land the kites (easier said than done, travelling backwards at 15mph with your head banging on the ground) or let go of them altogether.

A quicker stop can be made with practice. It involves basically the same manoeuvre but made at more speed and with more aggressive steering of the buggy. The main thing is to try steering the kite slightly more behind you at the top of the wind window and to do it fractionally (but fractionally) earlier, at the same time turning the buggy more aggressively upwind into a skid. At speed you slide the buggy to a stop facing upwind. Trying the fast stop means stopping with more power in the kite for you to lean against and hence there is more possibility of being pulled backwards out of the buggy. You'll need to get the kite to a minimum power position as quickly as possible once you've stopped or it may power up again.

Once you've mastered the power stop, why not try a few power skids, the buggy equivalent of the hand-brake turn? You're probably going to end up doing a few inadvertently anyway, taking into account the effect of apparent wind as described earlier, that moment when the kite is flying so far downwind of you that you are pulled sideways in a big skid, fighting with opposite lock on your steering. It's easier on sand needless to say but perfectly possible on grass, especially when it's wet or the ground soft. To skid:

- drive the buggy on a reach across the wind with the kite powered-up and locked in position at 45 degrees to the ground on the edge of the wind window.
- begin flying the kite up the window and slightly behind you as for a power stop. At the same time slam the buggy into an aggressive upwind turn and immediately reverse lock your steering.
- keep the kite slightly less behind than you would to come to a stop and then turn it back towards the edge of the window it was on, flying across the top of the wind window.
- move the kite into position on the edge of the window and, as it begins to power up again, let the buggy get going downwind a little then neutralise your steering to allow it to pick up speed before steering back onto a cross-wind reach.

Your ultimate sanction for stopping is to drop your control handles, releasing the kite and its pressure and allowing the buggy to roll gently to a stop. Or you turn the buggy upwind to stop sooner. This is normally not at all recommended as your kite and flying lines could seriously injure someone else on their way to ground and will almost certainly be in an incredible mess when you eventually catch up with them again wherever they've blown away to. And until the kite can be immobilised it represents a danger to other site users, including other buggy drivers. It may take out anyone in the immediate vicinity on its way to ground. Apart from all the safety issues, your quad-line set spaghetti-d around someone else's axles or flying lines is normally considered a gross breach of buggy etiquette.

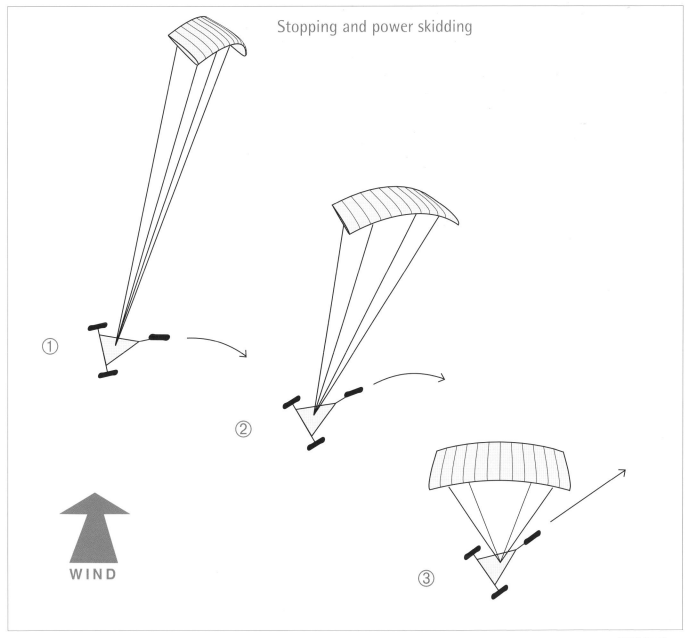

The five stages of gybing

WIND

① ② ③ ④ ⑤

Flexifoil Blade and Bullet kites now come fitted as standard with an emergency safety leash, as described in the set-up procedures. This means that can now let go completely of your handles, safe in the knowledge that the kite will firstly de-power and, secondly, return to ground with minimal risk to yourself and others. Recovering and relaunching the kite afterwards is relatively simple Always attach your safety leash(es) before buggying and practise your emergency drill before you have to use it for real. Even the pro pilots can get into difficulty and they would be the first to stress the importance of safe buggying.

You may occasionally be forced to stop if your kite becomes waterlogged, either from rain or some unintentional landings on the wet part of the beach. No option here: you must take it back somewhere dry, dry it out thoroughly and empty any sand out from inside before relaunching.

Gybing

This odd word, borrowed from sailing, means turning the buggy through 180 degrees to go back the way you came which, no matter how good a time you're having buggying off into the sunset, you will have to do sometime. And thinking about it, it's not at all obvious. The kite's in front of you, nicely powered-up, what do you do with it next to get it back to the other side of the wind window without being pulled out of the buggy? Which way do you turn the buggy anyway, up or downwind?

You can turn up or downwind but upwind is an advanced technique so we'll concentrate on the downwind version. Like all manoeuvres, it's one that needs good timing and adjustment all the way through. The first and most important thing you'll need to adjust is your forward speed. You can't really learn how to turn going in at full speed and you'll need to lose some before you go in. The main thing to remember is always to turn downwind, towards the kite. You need to turn the buggy as quickly as possible. Actually turning the buggy is very easy as your feet are steering directly through the front wheel. There's no counter steering against the pull. See oposite:

① and ② You are driving your buggy on a cross wind reach with the kite powered-up and locked at 45 degrees to the ground. Start steering the buggy slightly upwind and the kite up the edge of the wind window towards the zenith. The power eases off a little and the buggy starts to lose speed.

③ You're ready to make your turn. Steer the kite back up the wind window to the centre, the leading edge pointing straight upwards. At the same time steer the buggy hard into the turn. You need to use full lock to bring the buggy round quickly.

④ As the buggy comes round 180 degrees and is pointing back the way you came, start steering the kite over to the other side of the wind window, the side you want to move towards.

⑤ Let the buggy get going again downwind slightly, then neutralise your buggy steer-ing and steer the kite to the correct position to lock it on the edge for your return reach. Be ready for the pull coming back on as the kite powers back up again.

There's a fine balance to strike to make a good turn. You must slow down beforehand but you've also got to make sure you go in with enough speed to get all the way through the turn or you risk being pulled out of the buggy. If the buggy stops moving then the moment when the kite powers up again is when you could be yanked face forwards out of and across your buggy.

As you make your downwind turn you come face on to the kite. If you travel too far downwind or too fast you will de-power the kite, causing it to deflate and start to fall from the sky. Two things are then likely to happen. Firstly, as the kite sinks your flying lines fall on the ground, you run over them with the buggy and, hey presto, 293 twists of line round your axle. Secondly, with no kite to pull it, the buggy slows down, the wind blows on the kite bringing tension back onto the flying lines, the kite re-inflates and the power kicks back in but now it's low down in the window, right in the power zone, and pulls you face forwards out of your buggy as it does so. If both of these happen then you're in big trouble as the kite will be almost impossible to control with its lines snagged round the axle. You will have to forget about the handles and try to retrieve and control the kite before you can sort out the mess. That's why it's important to try and get the buggy round its turn as quickly as you can.

Most people's problems with turning arise from lack of forward speed going in or from going too far downwind in the turn. With practice you'll be able to make your turns faster, keeping more power in the kite, and clearly you're going to need to practise turning to both sides, for your own convenience and in case of needing to take emergency avoiding action. Soon you'll be ready for some power turns which come a lot easier if you've fully mastered the power stop and slide. The difference here is that you're going to be sliding downwind, towards the kite:

- you are driving the buggy fast on a cross-wind reach. Steer the kite quickly up the edge of the window and to a position high in the window, leading edge pointing straight up.
- as you do so, slam the buggy into a full 180 degree turn, steering the kite over to the other side of the window to its locked' position where it will quickly power up again.
- reverse your buggy steering to counter the pull, putting it into a skid. Then quickly neutralise the buggy steering to accelerate away from the turn on an opposite reach, bringing the kite to its 45 degree angle to the ground.

The trick is to be quick with the kite so that the moment when you are face on to the kite and it is powered-up passes quickly. The kite will still, briefly, be behind you, this time with more power. You will be powering into the corner and it will be more difficult to turn the buggy so you will need good leg strength and quick feet to whip the buggy round fast. And with more power you will need to lean against the kite, making a lot of work for your lower back and upper body. The advantage of a power turn is that, if you get it right, obviously it's much faster and you lose less ground downwind.

Getting upwind

Once you've established enough control over what you're doing in the buggy to be able to reach backwards and forwards across the wind you will want to learn how to turn that into steady upwind tacking, either for racing or simply to avoid the dreaded long walk back. However well you learn to get upwind it is always going to be slow progress and you must be patient and prepared to work the kite and buggy to get where you want to go.

Getting back upwind is the hardest thing to learn as a buggy driver so if you find it difficult at first, stick with it because patience will definitely bring its rewards. Initially, as you learn to drive, you will find that your reaches take you gradually downwind. To get back upwind you will need to steer more aggressively with your feet, trying to keep the buggy pointing slightly upwind on each tack, at the same time being less aggressive with the kite. You need to keep the kite less powered up by keeping it higher than normal on the edge of the wind window. If the kite is too low in the sky or too powered-up you will find it hard to gain ground. And there's that apparent wind factor to consider also. Again there's a fine balance to

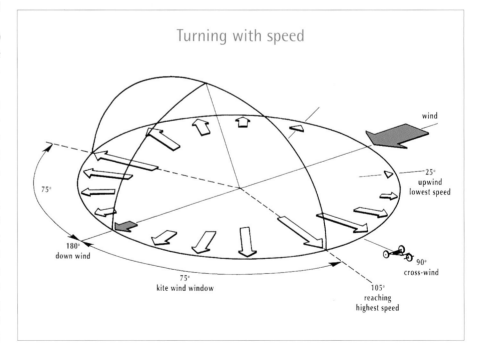

Turning with speed

wind

25°
upwind
lowest speed

90°
cross-wind

180°
down wind

75°
kite wind window

105°
reaching
highest speed

75°

achieve because if you're travelling too slowly and haven't got enough power you'll also find it difficult. This is particularly so during the turn at the end of each tack. The turns are made downwind as normal and if you lose speed or stop you're going to have to give up some of your hard won ground upwind going slightly downwind to get the buggy moving again. You need to make the turns as tight as possible, if you can, steering a little more upwind just before the turn and turning through more than 180 degrees to get on another upwind tack.

If it sounds difficult that's because it is. But once you've mastered this you've got a full hand of buggy manoeuvres and a whole adventure playground of kite powered possibilities will open up for you.

Essential and optional buggying equipment

There's an awful lot more to good buggying than simply having a kite and a buggy. There are all sorts of other bits and pieces you might want to have that will make your buggying easier and more enjoyable. But it's not simply a question of fun; first and foremost there's the safety aspect, protecting yourself and others from the worst case scenario because you're playing with big power and anything can happen. When you see a race driver fully kitted-out nowadays, ready

▶ Top: Crash helmet and sun glasses
▶ Middle: Knee pads
▶ Bottom: Elbow pads

to race in all weathers, they may have as many as 50 different extra accessories on top of the essential kite and buggy.

Essentials:

- crash helmet protects from hitting other objects or being hit by the buggy.
- strong shoes; your feet take a lot of wear and tear.
- knee, elbow and wrist guards, protecting vulnerable joints from knocks and hard landings.
- suitable eyewear, sunglasses to protect from ultra violet and glare but more likely goggles to keep sand and spray out of your eyes.
- gloves.
- ground stake for immobilising your kite.
- splash guard (comes as part of standard Flexifoil buggy package).
- safety leash (comes as part of standard Flexifoil traction kite package).

Optional:

- waterproof clothing, some kind of a spray suit.
- thermal inner clothing.
- face guard to protect from spray (fits onto the helmet).
- scarf to protect from spray. This and the face guard can help prevent some nasty skin infections you pick up from some dirty coastal sites.
- ankle straps with a ground stake sheath.
- wind meter.
- harness and harness loop which are invaluable if you want to buggy for long periods or in really big winds. You should not con-

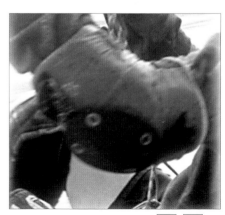

sider trying a harness until you have fully mastered the basic elements of kite buggying.

- large ground stake (dog stake or other) for keeping several different-sized kites immobilised but ready to fly at one time on days of changeable winds.
- line equaliser for quick testing if your flying lines have stretched and by how much.
- chest protector.
- shin guards.
- beach tent or cabana to store spare equipment in and to get out of the wind for a rest when you can't always take your vehicle onto the beach.
- a back rest because it can be very hard work for your lower back.
- foot peg straps which will help stop your feet bouncing off the pegs as you go over bumps or round turns.
- a speedometer so you know how fast you're going.
- a compass to know which direction.
- rear kit bag to carry spare kite and lines.
- extra wide soft sand tyres.
- extra wide axle to reduce sideways skid.
- buggy belt to strap yourself in for some jumps on the sand dunes or simply to hold you in under extreme power (this can be extremely dangerous).
- tandem kit for attaching another buggy to the rear of your buggy (there is theoretically no limit to how many buggies could be attached in a tandem).
- teflon-based lubricant (bike chain spray) for maintenance of the bearings.

And that's without looking at all the things like spare control handles or bars and flying lines, spare buggy parts, toolkit, sailcloth repair tape and kits, flying line sleeving and splicing kit..

It goes without saying that kite buggying is not really a sport you can go and do using public transport, you'll be needing a car or small van at the very least.

▶ Top: Goggles

▶ Middle: Spray guard

▶ Bottom: Wind meter

◀ Carving up the high water in a buggy

Other
Land Based
activities

ONCE THE BASIC PRINCIPLE of kite traction for wheeled transport became established, curiosity naturally drove people to experiment with various other options. Some things were obviously off limits, such as biking, the ability to steer with your hands being somewhat crucial and in any event the centre of balance being too high. Skateboarding is an obvious contender but is just too fast and unstable; there's not enough board to really lean against and again the centre of gravity is high.

Kite landboarding

Like a big, off-road skateboard, landboards (also known as mountain or all-terrain boards) are great fun on any hard beach or big inland open space with reasonably smooth terrain, playing fields being the obvious option. A beach with its advantages of space and smooth wind is what you really want to help you learn quickly. Confined spaces, bumpy surfaces and lumpy winds can make life very tricky taking into account the relatively small board surface to grip and high centre of gravity. As usual you'll need a very big space, away from other people and obstacles, with plenty of room downwind in case you are pulled forward.

The same safety equipment as for buggying is recommended, with even more emphasis on the elbow, wrist and knee guards. What you won't want to begin with is a harness

◀ *The latest craze: kie landboarding*

because if you are pulled over forwards, the hook and its fitting could cause you injury pushing back against and into your abdomen. Later on you might decide to use a harness and it will certainly help get the centre of pull lower down hence reducing wasted effort, which means faster, more efficient boarding.

What was very much a minority activity in the traction kite scene as recently as 2001 is now one of the fastest growing. It's easy to understand. Firstly, there's now 20 years or more of skateboard and roller blade culture in the UK, people are much more interested generally in all those board, skate and surf sports. The same can be said of power kiting too, bringing two powerful movements together in one sport. And there's a third factor. Kiteboarding (on water) has become an international phenomenon but getting the equipment together that you must have to kiteboard safely doesn't come cheap.

Kite landboarding offers a lot of the same sensations – speed, power, jumps, adrenaline on a vastly lower budget. Not least you'll need a much smaller kite to get you moving fast on a landboard than on a kiteboard because the friction from those four small wheels is much less than that of the flat hull or hard edge of a kiteboard working into the water. And there's no need for expensive water relaunch capability for your kite either. Not only that, the skills you learn in kite landboarding will be very useful when you decide to take it all out onto the water. The standard of the boards being manufactured today has developed almost as fast and far as their water counterparts. Land,

mountain and ATB boarding without a kite has been around for a few years anyway, it's not as though the whole thing started completely from scratch yesterday.

As before, you'll be better off learning in a light to moderate wind where things will happen slower. You can afford to be much less powered up than for a buggy, especially on hard, flat sand, as the resistance from a mountain board is very low. Use a smaller kite to begin with as there will be less lateral pull and you should find it easier to stay up on the board. Tacking and getting upwind are the objectives.

Most boards are basically flat, curving up at front and rear tips, with a grip mat on the deck for the feet. They have cushioned, neoprene foot strap bindings which obviously help with leverage, just as they do in kiteboarding and windsurf. It's arguably better to learn without the bindings, mastering the basics before you start fixing yourself to the board.

There are two basic landboard concepts. Three-wheeled boards have their single wheel at the rear and cannot reverse, making them a better option for downhill (without a kite). You'll need to learn to gybe a three wheeler (in the same way as you do a windsurf board or a directional kiteboard) if you want to turn round and they can't go in reverse. Four-wheeled boards are able to go in both directions, like a Twin Tip board for kiteboarding (see later). Just as Twin Tips have made learning to kiteboard a much easier prospect for legions of newcomers to that sport, so the four-wheel landboard has become the essential tool for kite landboarders, eliminating the compulsory gybe but also opening up a whole new range of trick possibilities.

"The new Flexifoil kite landboards have a noticeable asymmetric shape giving extra heel support, better control and improved steering under kite power."

Mike Shaw, Flexifoil UK Sales Manager

The Flexifoil landboard range

Flexifoil International manufactures a complete range of four-wheeled kite landboards, each adapted to a specific performance requirement and skill level. The boards were designed by specialist company in that field, G2A, in association with and distributed by Flexifoil, to maximise potential sales through Flexifoil's huge and established dealer list as well as through other specialist land, mountainboard and adventure sports shops. G2A are experts in working with carbon, composites and moulding. They're also keen power kiters and when they came up with the new board design it was a logical next step for them to take it to the experts in taking power kiting to the people, Flexifoil.

  Apart from some radically cool deck and base (underside) decos, all three have advantages and features specific to kiting which

▶ *Top: Flexdeck*

▶ *Middle: Airdeck*

▶ *Bottom: Kava deck*

set them apart from existing landboards. Most striking is the innovative, asymmetric and ergonomic deck shape to allow greater heel pressure and easier tracking upwind. Not only do the decks curve slightly up towards the front and back tips, viewed from above they have a cut-away frontside edge with the backside edge curving equally outwards giving them a distinctive, convex arched shape as you will see from the photos. They are purpose built for kite landboarding (and not really designed for conventional landboard downhilling) and all three models have tough wood, fibre glass composite decks, 39cm axle width, strong five-spoke nylon wheel hubs, easy kick-off footstraps and come with a coil ankle leash as standard. In fact the wheels, trucks and bindings are pretty much as you'd find on a standard landboard. The leash means that when you crash, your board won't disappear down the beach and won't present a possible risk to other landboarders.

The Flexdeck is a great all-purpose landboard that is excellent for beginners but which has the performance to interest more adventurous and experienced riders. It is great for jumping and gives an all-round smooth and well-balanced ride. It has an intermediate wheel base length (92cm), skate trucks and 20cm tyres, all of which make it an excellent board for carving, jumping, running and riding. Fully fitted out it weighs in at 7kg.

Next up is the radical trick machine landboard, the Airdeck. At 82cm it is short and highly manoeuvrable with touch-sensitive steering. It's the ideal board for the more advanced rider who's looking for that bit of extra buzz to be had once you get into tricks and jumping. It's equipped with the same 20cm tyres and skate trucks but its smaller size and lower weight (6.7kg) means less drag in the air, maximising air time to make more radical tricks such as spins, grabs and flicks easier. There's even a kiteboard style grab handle mounted in the centre of the deck for greater grab and board-off technicality and creativity, taking kite landboarding into the realms of pure freestyle.

The third member of the Flexifoil landboard squad is the Kava deck, the longest and largest of the boards at 106cm wheelbase. The Kava deck is designed mainly for long-distance cruising and for racing. Its innovative steering springs give a supremely well-balanced and controllable ride even at high speeds. The longer wheelbase, deeper channel truck and slightly larger 23cm tyre make for smooth riding, minimal rolling resistance and greater comfort on uneven ground. With that preloaded convex shape it compensates for rider power right through the board and is ideal for long runs, carving, enduro and safari type trips.

Your complete Flexifoil kite landboard package includes the deck, trucks, footstraps, deck grip pads, wheels, safety leash, a neat tool kit, all the required fittings, an instruction manual, product registration card and a Flexifoil sticker. If any of these items is missing from your pack contact your local dealer or Flexifoil International immediately. You will need to mount the footstraps, trucks, wheels and leash yourself,

◀ *Getting some air on a Kava deck*

preferably in your garage or house, you could ask them to put it all together in the shop (depending on how busy they are). Once you've got it fully assembled and you're wearing the appropriate protective gear you're ready to start experiencing the big buzz of kite landboarding.

Getting started

Your final check before getting on the board is to see if you are regular or goofy. This determines which way you prefer to stand and, in particular, which foot you place forwards when you stand to ride a board. If you don't know, have a friend shove you in the back. Whichever foot you use to save yourself is your lead foot and the other the supporting foot. Goofy is right foot forward, regular left foot forward. Start off by going towards your good side to make it easier. Now set up your board, as for a buggy start, pointing downwind across the window, at 45 degrees to the wind direction, towards your good side:

- launch your kite and fly it up to the minimum power position at the zenith.
- you will need to approach the board from one side or the other. From upwind means you can see where you're putting your feet better, important if you've got bindings to get into, but could trip over the board if pulled by a gust. From downwind means no tripping over but not seeing where you put your feet so well. Try from upwind first and see which you prefer.

- you will need to bring the kite down the edge of the window you want to move towards, taking care not to bring the kite too low and risk being pulled off as a result. The board should then move towards the kite and keep moving towards it as long as you keep the kite there. There's a lot of body work to be done, balancing and levering against the kite and you'll need a good flexed position, knees and arms slightly bent.
- start by steering slightly downwind to get some momentum before gradually easing yourself onto a cross-wind reach. Do this by transferring weight slightly onto your heels.
- you can slow down any time by taking the kite higher in the wind window but you'll need to shift your balance to allow for the reduced pull.

Remember that apparent wind factor we explained earlier. It will affect you here just like on a buggy and you will need to either adjust the board's steering or move the kite slightly to compensate. All being well it shouldn't take much time before you learn to hold a cross wind reach fairly comfortably. Just like buggying, that will bring another couple of issues up; those of turning and turning round.

You'll quickly notice, and you'll already know if you've come from a skateboard / mountainboard background, that when you lean either forwards or backwards on the board the effect is to turn it. If you're riding regular, leaning forwards will turn you to your right and leaning back will turn you left (vice versa for goofy riders). It's the land equivalent of front and backside carving on

a kiteboard or snowboard. Leaning backwards against the pull of the kite feels more natural whereas shifting your weight forwards with the pull to ride more frontside feels less secure. Experiment at first when you are not too powered-up, with small 'weaves' whilst running in one direction, gently slaloming the board between an imaginary set of cones. Keep the kite relatively high on your frontside carves to avoid having to lean too far forward. As your skill level and confidence grows you'll be able to gradually carve faster, harder and more aggressively, using more sustained kite power through the turns, compensating with your body strength and position.

As far as turning the board round 180 degrees goes you've got two choices. The first involves turning the board like a directional kiteboard or windsurfer, what's known as jibing. This is the old fashioned way of turning round (the only way on a three wheeled board without stopping and getting off) which, in a neat twist, has become a cool trick as it involves coming out of the turn riding frontside. Confused? Let's talk you through it. You're on a good straight run across the wind:

- transfer your weight to your toes and the board will begin to turn downwind, towards the kite. Go carefully, not too much weight too quickly. You are aiming to do a wide, carving, downwind turn. It might be worth carving slightly upwind just beforehand so as not to lose ground downwind.
- as you begin to turn the board, fly the kite up the edge of the window, turning it to

point the other way and gradually bringing it across the high part of the window to begin pulling you in the opposite direction, keeping tension on the flying lines.

- keep the weight on your toes as the board comes round 180 degrees.
- bring the kite to the appropriate position and lock it on the edge of the wind window. The kite will power up again and you will accelerate forwards, back the way you came.
- keep your weight over your toes, leaning slightly forward, flying the kite over your left shoulder (right shoulder for goofies).

It's all a question of timing and the more you practise the better your timing will be and you'll be able to make the whole thing in one sweeping movement. Don't go for it too powered-up at first but aim to keep the board moving all through the turn, as in a buggy gybe. If you do stop it will be difficult to keep your balance and power up again riding frontside. The advantage of this type of turn is that you keep moving all through the turn. The disadvantage is that you're now flying over your lead shoulder with your back to the kite and your weight forwards. It needs good balance and feel for the kite and will require some practice to get right. You'll need to turn round again or make a neat transition (a small jump with a half rotation of the legs to quickly switch the board) to get back to riding front on to the kite again. To make that frontside turn you'll need to make the same movements with the kite but

▶ *Getting some air on a Flexdeck*

reversed. The tricky bit might be working the board with your front foot to initiate the turn and shifting your balance completely from front to backside as you drive through it.

But a four-wheeled board, such as the Flexdeck, Airdeck and Kava, as we mentioned, is more like a Twin Tip kiteboard for water; it's symmetrical, so you can take advantage of its reversability when it comes to turning round. Gybing is a skill and takes some learning. You can speed up the delivery of your fun by getting going Twin Tip style while you take your time learning to gybe and ride frontside later. All you really need do is to slow down, stop, then power up again in the opposite direction:

- as you ride along bring the kite up the wind window where it will act as a brake, slowing you down. Shift your weight slightly to the centre of the board.
- fly the kite across the top of the wind window, turning it to point the other way. The board stops, bring your weight over onto your 'good' foot so you are now leading with your 'bad' one.
- as you bring the kite down the other edge of the window it will power up again and you can lock it at the appropriate place for your return reach. It's all in the timing again and practice will make for neater and more aggressive changes of direction.

Whichever way you're doing it, with practice you'll be able to make your turns faster and more aggressive, losing less power and speed. Tricks such as jumps and power slides can be done, especially once you start using bindings.

Stopping:

The simplest way to stop your landboard is, as explained, to steer the kite up to the zenith and keep it there while you slow to a stop. There's a way of stopping more quickly, similar to the way you stop a buggy

- you are reaching across the wind at reasonable speed. Start steering the kite up the edge of the window towards the top of centre wind window.
- as you do so, start applying pressure on the board with your heels to turn the board upwind, keeping the kite high in the middle of the wind window pointing straight upwards where it will brake your forward speed.
- lean slightly against the pull of the kite to stop your board. Keep the kite up at the zenith with minimum power.

With practice you'll be able to make the stop much more aggressive, moving the kite slightly earlier and more quickly. Be careful not to get the kite too far behind you or too quickly or too low down, all of which could lead to you being pulled backwards off the board.

Practise up this range of basic landboard manoeuvres until you're really confident. Think about taking a course at one of the many power kite schools there are now; it could well help speed up your learning processes. You'll need at least two sizes of kite if you want to landboard a lot, something for light winds, something smaller for medium to strong winds. You'll be amazed at the speed and aggressive carving you'll be able to achieve, leaning hard and hand dragging like a kiteboarder. In time you'll be ready to start going for some jumps and more complex direction transitions. Whatever level you aim to landboard at remember to always attach your kite and board safety leashes.

Snowkite

No university degrees handed out for guessing what this is all about. It seems fairly obvious that most things you can do on a waterboard or skis you should be able to do on a snowboard. After all, as the experts have been keen to point out, snow is simply frozen water.

Snowkiting is an area which, considering its potential, like landboarding, had lagged behind somewhat compared with buggying and then later on kiteboarding. The huge surge of interest in all forms of traction possibility during the last five years has given snowkiting its chance to emerge into the public gaze and awareness. In fact, given the slowness with which the medium has been exploited until recently, arguably the fastest progress is currently being made by the ice and snow kite freaks. As it stands, now there is an established winter competition tour in Europe and a series of events in the United States which are helping give the scene its momentum in terms of R&D, skill levels, exposure and encouraging new people into the sport. Competitions tend to take one of two possible formats: freestyle (similar to kiteboard freestyle) and racing. Freestyle is all about tricks, transitions, big airs and fluid riding. Racing is quite simply finding the

fastest rider from A to B. With the growth in market similar to that experienced by kiteboarding a couple of years ago, manufacturers have been encouraged to design specific snowkite equipment (boards, wings, etc.) knowing that the sales volumes they need to make such projects viable are starting to arrive.

The snowkite scene is really buzzing nowadays but there's nothing all that new about it. Back in the 70s, around the time Merry and Jones were developing their Flexifoil concept, two Swiss skiers, Andreas Khun and Dieter Strasila, were experimenting with old parachutes they'd bought secondhand from NASA, to see if they could be used to get up slopes not served by the chair lifts to ski back down. They called it paraskiing. Later they used parapentes to achieve the same thing but with the added possibility of parapenting down or, better still, flying in and out of a snowkite spot on a parapente. That's probably one reason why a number of parapente manufacturers have now got involved in manufacturing ram air snowkiting and other traction wings.

Ram air kites have been the most popular choice for snowkiting until recently, largely because of their extra manoeuvrability and the autonomy factor (you technically don't need a helper for the launch and landing phases). But increasing numbers of inflatable or tube kites (see Chapter 6) are being seen on the snow now with some inflatables being designed specifically for snowkiting.

It has taken almost 30 years for Khun and Strasila's idea to happen but nowadays there are increasingly large numbers of riders on the snow each winter using ever more

sophisticated equipment. And the skill levels have developed enormously with it. Riders are trying many of the water freestyle tricks and huge jumps. But remember, although snow is just frozen water it is a good deal harder and less forgiving. There's a risk of serious injury, to those associated with both skiing and power kiting. Always ride safely and use appropriate safety leashes and other devices where these are fitted.

There's a lot of attraction in snowkite as a great winter alternative to kiteboard, if you aren't lucky enough to have the kind of lifestyle that allows you to go chasing the sun every winter. That said, while Europe generally is quite well blessed with snow covered adventure playgrounds in the Alps, Pyrenees, Dolomites and Scandinavia not everyone has the kind of access to appropriate snow slopes and flats as they do water. British snowkiters are almost certainly looking at a trip to mainland Europe for their thrills and spills. As with most forms of skiing and snowboarding, Britain's main ski spot, the Cairngorms, just isn't reliable enough. If you've booked your ten days off work you don't want to be let down by the conditions.

If you do get into snowkiting you will need to develop three sets of skills to be able to ride safely. Kite skills, board or ski skills and finally, you will need to develop a sense for the mountains and snow. The risks are enormous, especially off-piste which is where most snowkiters will be, kites being banned at many recognised ski stations because of the potential safety risk they present to other skiers and boarders. There is a risk of

avalanches or of falling badly, but also the risk of the weather closing in and cutting off your route or simply losing yourself in the wide open spaces. And that's all in addition to the normal risks presented by the flying of large traction kites and the wearing of skis or snowboards. You will need to be well protected and well prepared. That means crash helmets, harness, warm clothing, goggles, gloves, food, drink, map, ice axe and some kind of GPS or avalanche rescue device.

Although Flexifoil hasn't yet turned its attention to designing a kite specifically for the snow, there are two ram air kites in the Flexifoil range, the Blade and Bullet, which are recommended for snowkiting. The Bullet is more suited to beginner riders because of its medium speed and stable handling. Also because, with a maximum size of 4.5 m^2, you're not going to be dealing with the bigger power that a 10.5 m^2 Blade has. The Blade, with its faster speed and harder, more consistent pull, is more for intermediate to advanced riders. On snow you can choose to ride with handles or with a control bar. The same arguments apply as before: using handles gives you greater mobility and manoeuvrability of the kite, using the control bar is simpler with more possibility for hands-free manoeuvres such as grabbed jumps.

The ideal spot for learning snowkite is a wide, open, flat expanse where the wind may be smoothest. Frozen lakes usually offer the best opportunities as these can extend for vast distances. If you're snowkiting in the mountains at altitude, be aware that the air is thinner and you may need more wind to get the power you want, but watch out for

wind surges! Generally speaking the friction on snow and ice is much less than on water and the power required to get moving needn't be too great. You'll also need to decide whether you want to ride a snowboard or with skis.

The snowboard's similarity to a twin tip kiteboard makes it a good choice for winter kiteboarders whereas people already into skis may well wish to stick with them. Learn without using the harness, flying smaller kites to begin with until you have completely mastered the basics, before you try attaching yourself to a bigger wing with much more power. Again, the best thing would be to go to a school and do a course; as usual it will accelerate your learning process. At present the best place to look for school contacts is in the kiteboard and power kite magazines or on the internet.

Getting started

If you've already had a go at buggying, landboarding or kitesurfing then nothing will be at all strange, other than the new medium. The basic principles are the same and for beginners there's a simple test you can do to determine which is the correct kite size. Launch your kite, put it at the zenith and if you can't walk backwards holding the kite there your kite is too big. Change down a size. Avoid going out over-powered. Inland wind, specially in the mountains, can be very gusty and if you're ripped out by a gust it could well mean the end of your session, day or even holiday. And don't overestimate your

ability; try to be honest, you'll learn quicker. Finally, whether you're using a control bar or handles, a board or skis, always, always attach your safety leash(es).

Establish a safe area downwind of at least two line lengths. Unroll your kite and either weight it down along the trailing edge (in moderate winds) or the upwind tip (stronger winds) with snow. In stronger winds you should set up near the edge of the wind window. If you're flying with handles, wind about four or five turns of the brake lines in,;if you're on a control bar pull the rear lines in as far as the stop, both of which will prevent the kite self-launching.

When you're properly ready to launch, let out the brake lines and slowly move backwards until the front of the kite starts to lift up and the kite inflates with air (or the downwind tip if using the other method). Pause at this point and allow the kite to inflate as much as possible before take off. You can launch the kite exactly the same way as described earlier in the book, allowing for yourself to be pulled some way forwards as the kite passes through the power zone of the window on its way up to the zenith. Learning to launch from and use the edge of the window can seem pointless but will in fact serve you well when it comes to riding out wind surges. If you are using a harness now is the time to hook in, before you get your skis or board on. Don't take your eyes off the kite for more than second at a time.

Be methodical about setting up and you'll avoid endless to-ing and fro-ing untwisting lines etc. Try some test launches and landings before you get onto your board or skis to make sure everything's ok.

To begin with you're going to get going downwind, just as in your buggy or on your landboard, before you start trying to work the edges of your skis or board and the kite position to hold a line across the wind, which is the ultimate aim of the learning phase. With your kite at the zenith and your skis or board on:

- bring the kite slowly down in front of you in the wind window, not too far, just enough to power it up and get you moving forwards. Be careful not to let the lines go slack as the kite will fold up and fall down the window, then pick up again viciously as the wind kicks back in. Try to dig the edges of your skis or board in to keep the line tension.
- if you want to try and accelerate fly a small 'S' pattern with the kite. Once you've got some speed up, the apparent wind factor will begin to apply and you should be able to lock the kite in position towards the edge of the window with constant power.
- while building the power in the kite you should also be trying to work the edges of your skis or board further and further round until you hit your 'reach' line, across the wind.

It all comes down to good synchronisation of these basic elements: holding a good line with your skis or board, acceleration and speed. At all costs avoid taking the kite behind you as this will almost certainly lead to an uncomfortable wipe-out. Without a doubt your first few runs will take you downwind but with practice you will be able to get back upwind, just as you can in the other land activities.

Across or downwind, there's also no doubt that at some stage you're going to need to slow down or stop without hurting yourself, preferably learning how to turn 180 degrees so you can make your return run back to your start point. Unless you skipped the earlier sections you'll already have guessed roughly what's involved in all these manoeuvres seeing as what we're basically doing is translating the same wind behaviour, kite principles and rider skills from one activity to another. To slow down and stop:

• dig your edge(s) in with heel pressure to turn slightly upwind.
• at the same time pull slightly on the upper tip of the kite to manoeuvre it back up the wind window towards the zenith. Again, be careful not to take the kite too far behind you or with any power.
• as the kite de-powers at the zenith you will gradually come to a stop.

The 180 degree turn or gybe, as the buggy and kiteboarders have it, is a combination of all the elements you would expect if you've already done any skiing or boarding and had some power kite experience or read the earlier sections of this book. If you're a snowboarder there's no problem; you're riding a twin tip that can go backwards and forwards like a four-wheeled landboard. That way you can stay in the more natural position, riding backside, leaning back digging the upwind

edge in. It's exactly the same manoeuvre with the kite as with the landboard, up the window to the zenith (careful not to let it get behind you), slow down to a stop and power up going back the other way, leading with your other foot. The same frontside option applies as does to the landboard, though, meaning you could choose to turn more like a skier, actually shifting to the other edge and turning round to lead with the same foot on the frontside edge but flying 'blind' over your leading shoulder. For a snowboarder a slalom is a series of back and frontside edge turns.

Turning round through 180 degrees on snow should, as in your kite buggy, always be done downwind. The turn is initiated with the board or skis and you will need to try and drive through the turn smoothly and as fast as manageable to avoid de-winding the kite. Likewise, try not to turn too wide for the same reason, going in with reasonable but not excessive power allowing you and the kite to get round comfortably:

- initiate the move with your board or skis by gradually bringing them flat and adopting a more upright body position, weight moving over towards the downwind edge of your board or skis. Bring the kite up the wind window towards the zenith
- with the kite at the zenith there will be a moment when you are flat on the skis or pointing downwind. Keep driving through the turn to avoid de-winding the kite. Bring your weight over the opposite edge of your skis to the one you were on / frontside edge of your board

- power the kite up again by bringing it over to the edge of the window you wish to move towards and slightly down the window, working the edge(s) of your skis or board with heel or toe pressure to complete the turn.
- as you come out of the turn on skis you will be leading with your other, upwind, foot flying front on to the kite and leaning back against the pull. On a snowboard you will now be riding on your toes, still leading with your good foot, but now leaning forwards and flying the kite over your lead shoulder.

With practice you'll soon be able to ski back and forward across the wind, get upwind, until you've fully mastered these basic elements. At that point you'll be ready to try some jumps, using the snow contours and wind currents to boost your airs, spotting your landings and carving up the snow. Although we haven't gone as far as jumps here you'll find a section on jumping in Chapter 6 following this that gives you the same kite manoeuvres. The rest is up to you. Please make sure that you're fully protected before you try jumping on snow, accidents can all too easily happen and you'll obviously have a few crashes during the learning phase. Enjoy your snowkiting but most of all, enjoy it safely.

Rollerblades

For the time being this one can still be filed under 'interesting but strictly minority'. But then that's what they said about kiteboarding and landboarding and look at them now...Rollerblading means low resistance, high speed and hard crashes. Not for the faint hearted, full safety equipment recommended, small kites only.

This is mostly done on a kind of mountain / landboard version of rollerskates or blades, using mountain or landboard wheels. One or two companies now manufacture these and you should try skate and kite retailers as a first suggestion. But if you find them difficult to track down you're looking at a DIY project. You can try conventional rollers on tarmac if you like but it's hellish fast and hurts a lot when you crash.

Blades and skates are a bit more like water skis and wakeboards in so much as you strap yourself in first and then launch the kite to power yourself up. That in itself presents dangers because if you get into difficulty you cannot detach yourself from them; you will have to deal with the kite somehow. Saying that, clearly the potential is there to go very fast with such low resistance and there's possibly more freedom of movement for jumps and tricks than with landboards. Time will tell.

Getting started
Start with a small kite, sufficient to get you moving until you have mastered the basics with a small kite don't attempt it with a

bigger one. Even so, being strapped in you don't want to launch the kite in centre window with full power so you need to set things up carefully. Work out your regular or goofy stance and go in that direction to begin with as you will be leading with one foot. Use a small kite in moderate wind and, as before, the first objective is to learn to ride backwards and forwards across the wind:

- set up the kite close to the edge of the wind window, on the side to which you want to go.
- put your blades or skates on along with your other safety equipment and get ready to launch the kite, pointing yourself slightly downwind to help get some momentum. Your feet should be parallel with your good foot slightly advanced.
- launch and fly the kite straight up the edge to the zenith, balancing your body to lever against any pull. If you move forward a little do not worry, taking the kite to the zenith will stop you again.
- now, bring the kite slowly down the edge of the wind window on the side you want to move towards. It will begin to power up and you will begin to move forwards. You will need to make lots of body adjustment to lever against the pull. Keep your knees bent, leaning back to lever against the kite.

Stopping

- take the kite up the edge of the wind window towards the zenith, pointing straight up. The kite will be flying slightly behind

▶ *Fast and dangerous — powered rollerblading*

▲ Leaning into it on blades

you and will act as a brake.

- turn your blades to point further upwind, so you're flying over your shoulder. You will quickly come to a stop.
- keep the kite at the zenith or land it right on the edge of the wind window.

An alternative to this of course would be to apply full reverse with your rear lines. This should de-power the kite immediately and you can turn the blades upwind whilst you reverse land the kite.

Turning is done the same way as usual, downwind, similar to a landboard, but you will eventually be able to carve tighter turns, the small size and light weight of the skates making it easier to get over onto the other edge. You will have to make a transition with your feet so that you're leading with your 'bad' foot. This means you can stay face on to the kite. Otherwise, to stay leading with your good foot, come out of the turn riding frontside, leaning forward and flying over your lead shoulder.

Getting big airs with tricks and gymnastics

If you get into getting your airs in a big way you'll be looking for two things: distance and hang time. The biggest officially recorded jumps have been of well over 100' (30 metres) and have been done with the help of full support and back-up teams, not to mention medical assistance on hand if necessary. Stories of even bigger training and accidental jumps abound, with varying degrees of amazing escapes, broken bones and sometimes more serious consequences. You can use big stacks of Flexis or big single traction

foils; both will do the job.

The basic idea of the tricks is to start actually using your hang time, in the same way that kiteboarders are doing, to hit some rotations or whatever. Like everything else try in moderate winds with some smaller airs to begin with. You will be landing on hard ground at speed. Build up power and size of your jumps gradually as you gain skill and confidence. Single and multiple rotations and somersaults are the general order. Be aware that any sizeable jump is going to result in a very heavy landing so you really do need to be fully protected with helmet, gloves, strong footwear and elbow, knee and wrist guards. It's very tiring and you won't be able to keep going too long. Especially as all your jumps will be taking you downwind

leaving you a stamina-sapping walk back upwind to your start point trying to keep you kite(s) at the zenith with no power.

Acknowledging the somewhat unhinged nature of the activity, try even so to take care with getting your airs, just like all your other power kiting disciplines, and minimise the risk to you and others. That way you'll enjoy your power kiting to the maximum.

▲ *Getting those big airs*

▶ *Time for some tricks*

Kites for
Sea and surf

"I switched to kiteboarding (from wind-surfing) for the big airtime. Combined with the bonus of less hassle, kiteboard-ing has the best bits of windsurfing times ten."

Chris Calthrop
Flexifoil sponsored kiteboarder

The information in this chapter is intended as a guide only. We strongly recommend that you take lessons from a fully qualified instructor BEFORE attempting to kiteboard.

THROUGHOUT THE SHORT history of the sport, there's been much learned discussion and disagreement about when and where exactly kiteboarding was invented. What's not disputed is that people have been experimenting with kite power on water for years and that the current explosion of interest in this new most radical of extreme sports is the result of a long and winding journey to arrive where we are now. The potential was obviously there if only the formula could be perfected. Flexifoil themselves experimented with the kite boat, *Jacob's Ladder*, and other earlier aquatic efforts.

Elsewhere in the world other people had tried water skis and with adapted buggies, floats fitted in place of the wheels. Of all these, Corey Roesler's 'Kiteski' rig, dual water skis with a large, framed kite and a motorised winding, recovery or relaunch system on a control bar, which was up and running in 1993, was the most workable and the closest to what we recognise today as kiteboarding, but not commercially successful. Ahead of his (and its) time in many ways and still very much involved with the water kite scene.

◀ *Kiteboarding: The ultimate wind/water buzz*
▶ *One of the original water men – Corey Roesler*

The general consensus nowadays seems to be that kiteboarding was actually done successfully first in the south of France, on the coast near Montpellier, some time around 1996 or 1997. From there it was exported, mainly by one man, Manu Bertin, to Hawaii, or more correctly Maui, to where the likes of legendary futuristic surfer Laird Hamilton and his group were also trying to make kiteboarding happen. This small group of power kiters and surf freaks used adapted surf boards and the kind of big wings that were about at the time. Those mostly, with one notable exception, consisted of big ram air wings such as the two-line Peels, four-line Skytigers and, soon to come, Blade. From France and Hawaii kiteboarding has now been successfully exported to dozens of countries around the world.

Clearly there was one big issue that had not really cropped up in kiting before to any great extent, other than in an experimental or demonstration sense: water relaunching. A big ram air wing is made with big vents along the front, which take in water just as effectively as air. The ripstop fabric is covered with a waterproof coating but after more than a few minutes, lying flat on the water the whole sail becomes waterlogged and impossible to relaunch without gathering it all up, swimming back in, drying it out and starting again. And there was another issue concerning getting back upwind. Early kiteboarders spent a lot of time carrying their gear back from downwind runs, a combination of not yet having the skill, nor the kind of wing or board that would make that possible.

The basic point was that, once again, activity was running ahead of product development and people were using what kites were available rather than some

specifically designed for the job. The Blade was an interim response to this with fewer vents along the leading edge and an eliptical shape and, to this day, in a light wind there's still very little to beat a big ram air wing. In other wind conditions, however, there's another system that has swept all before it in both the competitive and commercial senses, filling the podium positions at nearly all the major kiteboarding events in the last few years.

In 1984, French brothers and mastermariners from Brittany, Bruno and Dominique Legaignoux, patented a system for putting sealed inflatable tube stiffeners in a single skinned sail that could be flown as a kite on two lines attached directly to the wing's tips, the inflatable sections rendering it effectively unsinkable. Like all great ideas it was very simple. The wing, though some way from the finished product, flew OK, pulled hard enough for the resistance of rider on water, and was, technically speaking, fully water relaunchable. The inflatable tube stiffeners, one along the leading edge and a series of vertical battens, have a dual function as frame and buoyancy.

The Legaignoux brothers always believed in the possibility of kiteboarding, trying many experiments themselves over the years, and when pioneer kiteboarders like Manu Bertin saw the potential they started using the kites. Within a couple of years inflatable kites had been fully adapted for kiteboarding and now command the entire market.

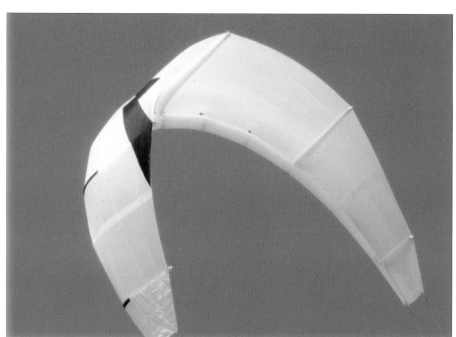

▲ Storm prototype in testing

As the inflatable wing idea started to win converts and market share, so, crucially, other big windsurf manufacturers getting into kiteboarding at that time, particularly opinion formers like Robby Naish and Neil Pryde and Pete Cabrinha, decided that inflatable was the way to go, bought a licence and started making kites. The rest, as they say, is history as a huge list of manufacturers have followed the inflatable route in the face of overwhelming competition success by and consumer demand for that type of wing, around 90% of the total market for kiteboard wings. That list now includes Flexifoil International who have bought a licence and produced the Storm, their own typically Flexifoil styled variant

of the classic inflatable wing.

Inflatable wings are very much the face of kiteboarding at present. Their tough build and the huge arched shape they take up in flight are very impressive and they really look the part. Since the wing has stiffeners there's no need for complex bridles and it's back to the simplicity of flying lines attached directly to the wing tips. Although they rule the market at present there's no telling how things will look in a few years. Kiteboarding is a very young sport generally and is developing so fast that, as far as the future is concerned, anything is possible.

Inflatable kites are increasingly sophisticated, which is not surprising with so many companies working on the same basic

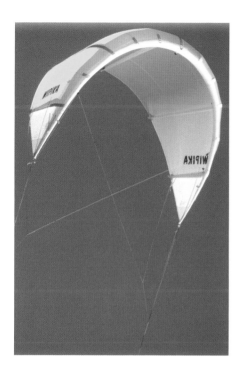

▲ The original: a Wipika inflatable kite

system, and many inflatables (LEIs – leading edge inflatables – in tech speak) can now be used with either two or four lines. Almost all water kites now have some kind of built-in de-power system, allowing you to adjust the pull while in motion by changing the angle of attack of the kite against the wind. Those that don't soon will because that's what the people want. They're all designed to make getting back upwind easier and needless to say they exist in a huge range of sizes, tending to be somewhat larger in surface area than equivalent powered ram airs to compensate for their arched shape. 'Competition' wings are very elongated, they have a very high aspect ratio giving them more power but making them more sensitive. Beginner inflatable wings tend to have lower aspect ratios and be more rounded in shape making them slower, more stable and generally easier to handle. In this respect they conform exactly to the normal principles of kites. What goes around has indeed come around again with this reversion to the control bar approach and reversion to two line flying, particularly for riders into wakeboarding and wave riding.

So too with flying line control systems, it's a control bar world out there on the water now that they have been successfully adapted to take two, four and even three-line set ups incorporating de-power and quick release safety systems. In kiteboarding, there are far bigger wings and power involved in the equation and harnesses are a must in order to be able to fly for any length of time. In the early days people used windsurf harnesses but now specific kite harnesses are being manufactured to deal with the different kind of loading and power kites give. Different length harness loops attached to the handles or control bar are used for different elements of riding and often carry the safety quick release. Nevertheless, there are times when it's better to be unhooked in case of getting into difficulties during a manoeuvre and being unable to unhook because of the pull of the kite..

Honourable mention should be made at this point of two other types of kite that have worked well and in one case continue to carve their own niche in the busy kiteboarding scene. The first is another Peter Lynn invention, called the C-Quad, a kind of hybrid with a flat single skin and series of carbon fibre battens and stiffeners. The other is an inflatable kite system, flat rather than arched, called the Manta concept, devised by Frenchman Eric Saurre. Being flat they developed pull without needing the bigger sizes of their arched counterparts. Some other manufacturers have tried similar wings, including a short-lived Flexifoil project called the Nexus. Both C-Quad and Manta-type kites have been good, efficient and safe performers and have played their part in the development of the sport. But frustratingly for them, both struggle for market share against the currently all-conquering arched inflatable wings.

The Storm

"If any kite would get me off Blades, it would be the Storm. It's more durable and has more style. That's the Flexifoil tradition of quality."

Danny Seales, Flexifoil team kiteboarder

The Storm was largely developed by Cambridge University aerodynamics graduate and recent addition to the Flexifoil design team, Henry Rebbeck, with input and assistance from Flexifoil founder Andrew Jones. Working from the original Legaignoux concept, it's a typical inflatable wing model. If the first Storm series had few specific aerodynamic features distinct from other inflatable wings, that's because Flexifoil hadn't yet tried to make any significant advances of their own to the general concept. That's all changed now with the release of the Storm 2 in 2003. The Storm 2 is the result of all the lessons learned from the original Storm's performance and shows the kind of technical refinements to both kite and control bar that have always marked Flexifoil out.

Being a big player in the kite industry is one thing. Competing with some of the heavyweights from the surf and windsurf industries is quite another. It's a potentially potent mix of past experiences, kites – boards – windsurf, coming together to drive the new sport forwards. Flexifoil have looked to one of their biggest strengths, that of taking power kiting to the widest possible market, when developing the Storm. There are plenty of beginner wings on the market and plenty more cutting-edge competition wings besides. The Storm fills a huge gap that exists for riders who've passed the elementary stage, aren't necessarily looking for a podium place on the pro tours but want the kind of wing that will do for them the kind of things the pro riders do: a wing that works well, that is simple and efficient to fly, that is fully water relaunchable, is built to a high standard, is good value and comes with the kind of full before and after sales advice and service that established companies with many years experience can offer. As luck would have it the Storm 2 is a great pro rider kite too and the Flexifoil pro team riders are taking it to new heights of competitive success for the company.

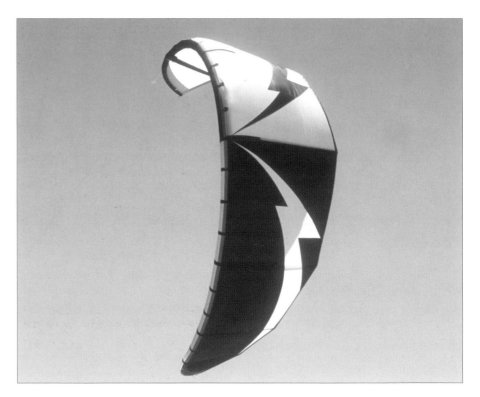

▲ *The Flexifoil Storm I production model*

There's been a lot of confusion, since they were first licensed, regarding curved inflatable wing sizes (it's different with ram airs and Manta type which are held flatter by their bridle structures), with different manufacturers using different, and quite legitimate, systems for measuring wing size. We're talking about the surface area of a wing type which, though flat when on the ground deflated, has a significant curve when inflated ready for launch and even more in flight. Although the Legaignoux brothers, who hold the inflatable wing patent, asked their licensees to end customer confusion by all working to the same

system from 2002 onwards, that system being the 'developed' also referred to as the 'projected' area, there's still no industry standard. Projected area is a calculation based on the sail area divided by a given factor. The other option is the 'flat' area – the area of ground covered by the wing when laid flat on the ground. The Storm's wingspan sizes are based on the flat area, the total surface area of the wing when laid flat. It all makes for a highly confusing secondhand market, to say the least.

To keep it simple, lets say the sail itself is made from tough ripstop polyester sailcloth which is well known for its durability and

Storm II specifications and sizes

Size	8	10	12	14	16	18	20
Flat surface area (m²)	8.0	10.0	12.0	14.0	16.0	18.0	20.0
Wingspan (m)	6.8	7.7	8.7	9.5	10.3	11.4	12.5
Aspect Ratio (As calculated by AR = Span²/Flat surface area)	5.5	6.0	6.2	6.4	6.6	6.8	7.0
Sail material	Ripstop Polyester						
Skill level (Beginner / Intermediate / Expert)	Intermediate/Expert						
Wind range - Top end (Knots) (based on 75kg rider)	30.0	27.0	25.0	23.0	21.0	19.0	18.0
Wind range - Bottom end (Knots) (based on 75kg rider)	19.0	16.0	14.0	12.0	11.0	9.0	8.0
Projected area (m²)	4.9	6.3	7.5	8.8	10.0	11.2	12.4
Equivalent Wipika sizing (m²) (As calculated by Flat surface area/1.36)	5.9	7.4	8.8	10.3	11.8	13.2	14.7
Flying lines (4 line set)	27m - 225 kg / 225 kg						

low stretch, the inflatable tubes from polyurethane and the pockets they fit into from polyester laminate. The new wing is built for durability in extreme conditions and is heavily reinforced at all the wear and tear points, notably the leading edge, trailing edge, line attachments and wing tips. Variable geometry means that all the wing sizes have the same handling characteristics. Its blended aerofoil geometry means it is smooth flying with huge de-power potential and big performance. It has multiple front and rear control line attachment points making it possible to tune the kite to different styles or conditions. The curved tips where the leading-edge tube becomes the tip batten reduce drag and increases speed and efficiency. The innovative rigid strut system linking the battens to the leading edge gives the wing a more solid frame enabling faster turns

and improved stability. Reactive tube technology and aerodynamic tube ends give great control in turbulent conditions, maximum recovery and reduced drag. All in all it's designed and built specifically for kiteboarding at its most efficient as the sport stands today. And for some time to come, almost certainly, as there's no sign yet of a totally convincing alternative to inflatable wings such as the Storm.

▶ Henry Rebbeck, one of the Storm's designers

Kiteboards

"Over a short time boards have changed loads. Mini-Directionals now come with two straps so you stand more in the centre, better for toe side riding. In flat water and strong wind the wake is the perfect toy. No gybing is a great plus point for twin tips, makes life a lot easier. Now everyone's trying to develop a mutant board with the best points of each."

Jason Furness, Flexifoil team kiteboarder

In the beginning of kiteboarding the kites were lacking a little and took a little time to adapt and the boards didn't exist at all. Most early kiteboard efforts were made on home-adapted surf or windsurf boards. All used some kind of foot bindings (like on a wind-surf board), essential for working against the pull of the kites. These were ok to get the sport up and running but weren't designed for the specific strains and loading of kite-boarding, specially when it came to the question of jumping, more specifically, the landings after jumps.

Of course it didn't take long for shapers and manufacturers from within the estab-lished sports of surf and windsurf, specially the latter, to start to look seriously at the new sport and kite specific boards soon started to appear, reinforced for kite power.

▲ *Early directional kiteboards*
▶ *The Flexifoil 'loose unit' kiteboard*

With its obvious link to windsurfing, most early kiteboards conformed to the direction-al principle. That is to say, they were made to go in one direction only. They were classic boards with plenty of volume to keep you afloat and a three fin ('Thruster') configura-tion at the rear for stability, course holding and control. Being mono-directional (for-wards only) meant that they had to be turned round for you to get back to your start point, the objective being to go back-wards and forwards across the wind, even upwind, skill level, board, kite and conditions allowing. Gybing was as much part of the essential requirement as beach starting, water relaunching and getting up on the board at all. Mainly because the only alter-native to gybing was to stop, put the kite at the zenith, take the board off and turn it to pint the other way and then water start again.

Just as some kiteboarders came to the sport from windsurfing, so others had had prior experience of wakeboard riding. Wakeboards are generally short and very thin, with the rider strapped into full foot bindings like on a snowboard and towed behind a power boat, playing and tricking on the boat's wake. It didn't take wakeboarders long to realise that you could use the same board with a big kite for power. You could even use a similar control bar to steer the kite and the standard 15 minute pay-per-tow has become a session as long as there's wind available.

Wakeboards made for a much trickier style of riding. Being much shorter and less voluminous meant that riders needed to be super powered-up to stay afloat. Wakeboards are also normally symmetrical lengthways, having fins at both ends to allow riders to lead with either foot during trick sessions. The implication for kiteboarding was immense. If the board could lead in either direction, no more turning round. To go back the other way you simply reverse your direction. The downside is that being so small, fast and radical and needing as much wing power as they do, wakeboards are not really suitable for beginners. Also, that being permanently strapped in to your foot bindings can make life a bit scary if you do get into difficulties.

What was required was a symmetrical board with sufficient volume for stability and fins at both ends for reversability. The boards duly started to appear during late 2000, the first developed by top French rider

▸ *Top: Wakeboard action*

▸ *Bottom: A custom twin tip board*

Franz Olry. 'Twin Tip' mania was born. Kiteboarding had finally established its individuality and differentness from windsurfing because you can't twin tip a windsurf board. With kite power, you want to turn round? You slow the board down almost to a stop and quickly, before it can sink, shift your weight and get the wing and it going in the opposite direction. You can still turn round if you want and ride on the other, frontside, edge for your return, but then you'll be flying over your shoulder with your back to the kite. In surf sports, frontside is what's in front of your toes and backside is what's behind your heels.

Improvements in design and construction over the years in both boards and kites now means it's perfectly possible to learn kitesurfing on a twin tip, without having to learn the gybe, and not surprisingly this is overwhelmingly the most popular type of board in the world today. But the sport is constantly developing and recent experiments have seen the appearance of wakeskateboards – a small tricky no-straps board, mini directionals, mutants, plus specialised boards for big wave, speed and distance kiteboarding some of which are going back to a more directional shape.

Kiteboarding can genuinely claim to be highly successful fusion of other sports and nowhere is this reflected more than in board shaping and design.

But the basic kiteboarding board family as things stand today is still directionals, wakeboards and twin tips. The general principle is:

▶ *Setting up your Storm II stages 1–6*

big board small wind, small board big wind. A big volume board in a big wind is just too much to handle and a small board in a small wind might well sink due to lack of flotation or power to keep it up. Mini twin tips and wakeboards are all the rage with experienced riders, and new mini directionals are giving the old format a new lease of life. Mini boards are great for fast action on the water and trickery in the air, giving rise to a radical skateboard style with lots of grabbed 'one-foots' and 'no-foots', that's jumping and holding the board, taking one or both feet out of the straps and back in again before landing (that kind of thing's not possible on a wakeboard because your feet are strapped in).

Having such a small board means you need loads of kite power to keep you going, meaning that most riders are very powered-up, another reason why they're not a great choice for beginners. The other general board principle is that you should learn on a bigger volume board that will be slower, more stable and keep you afloat better. That means light to moderate winds, too. Small, boards and big winds are not for beginners.

With the change in style of boards has come a change in style of riding, too. Where ,the big volume directionals are great for planing, small twin tips and specially wakeboards are ridden much more aggressively on the edges. Competition riding, which is the inspiration for so much of the media coverage and public interest, really only exists in two formats, at least on the major tours: Freestyle, free riding with the emphasis on tricks and fluid riding; Hang Time, about who can stay up in the air longest (not nec-

essarily the biggest jump).

Board shaping for kites is now big business and most of the big surf and windsurf manufacturers have ranges of dedicated kite boards distinct from their other products. Same with the fins which play such a vital role in controlling the board. Board evolution is by no means complete;, on the contrary, in many ways it's only just beginning and there's talk of new revolutionary shapes that enable you to ride with no side slide. With a sport that's so young and speed of development so rapid, anything is possible. There are dozens of manufactures and dozens more custom board shapers out there aiming to make it so.

You'll be faced with a bewildering choice if you start looking around at the number of different board models on the market. That's another reason why it's a good idea to go to a kiteboard school. That way you can not only test out one or two models, you can build up a much better picture of your level and what kind of board is best adapted to your needs whilst you learn and before you spend your money. Go to the spots and talk to the riders, ask their advice. Do a little techno surfing on the internet where there's a vast amount of manufacturer and rider information available. Don't be suckered into buying equipment that's beyond your skill level as you'll just have a hard time and risk killing your interest off for life. You can always trade up later or keep the original to lend a friend to help them get started.

Setting up an inflatable kite wing

As you'd expect, being part of the very well-developed surf industry with its acute sense of corporate identity, merchandise, paraphernalia and giving good value, when you buy a Storm II it comes in a logo-d, heavy duty custom storage bag. This bag is big enough to carry your kite in a temporary pack-down state, leading edge deflated but battens inflated. It's not recommended that you leave your battens inflated any length of time (no more than overnight).

Inside your carry bag you'll find a big pump for inflating the leading edge and battens, a moulded carbon-composite tapered ergonomic control bar fitted with a de-power and safety systems, a pre-stretched heat-treated colour-coded quad line flying line set appropriate for the size of wing you're buying, a product registration card, a bladder repair kit and some sheets of sail repair cloth, plus a full instruction manual. If for any reason any of this equipment is not in the bag you should contact your dealer or Flexifoil International direct. Try to remember, as you unroll the sail for the first time, how it was rolled to leave the factory so that you can do the same when you pack it away each time. You may want to try this once at home but you're going to need to know the full procedure for when you get out on the beach, lake or river side. Take a look at the diagrams ① to ⑥ which will help make sense of it all. Memorise and follow the step by

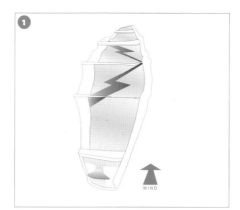

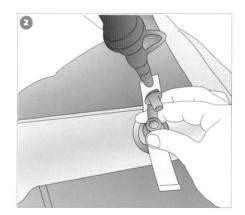

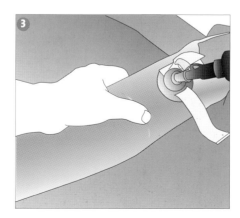

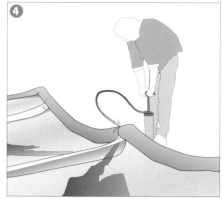

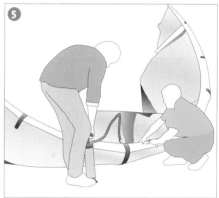

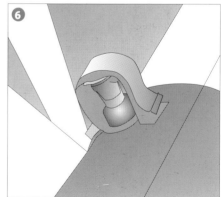

step preparation instructions to the letter.

If this was the start of a boarding session, now would be the moment to stop and put on your final pieces of safety equipment: crash helmet, harness and buoyancy or flotation aid. You might want to get used to this anyway whilst you're learning to fly the kite as that's the way it's going to be when you come to do it for real. To begin with, though, get used to flying the wing without your harness until you've fully mastered flying it. It's a completely different experience flying a big kite wing with your movement restricted by your wetsuit, harness etc. Especially built kiteboarding wetsuits and harnesses are now produced are designed with the extra flexibility of the articulations required by kiteboarders in mind.

The next stage will be to unwind your flying lines. Riders tend to use lines between 25 and 40 metres, longer in light to moderate wind and shorter (20 metres) in strong wind. As you will be learning in light to moderate winds you should have a line set of 35 to 40 metres long. The lines must be the appropriate strength for the size of your wing and wind, taking into account that when you use a kite on water there is about 30% more strain on the flying lines than when flying on land. This is due to the extra resistance of the water against your board and body. In fact your lines will be made of high-quality Dyneema with its advantages of low stretch, low weight, low diameter (in relation to equivalent strength nylon or polyester) and good slipperiness.

▶ *Weighting down your Storm*

Unlike your ram air traction kites the lines will be of equal strength as the weight and pull loadings are more evenly distributed between front and back. They will be sleeved at each end to prevent snapping where knots are tied (Dyneema has a low melting point so friction from knots would cause the lines to cut through themselves at the knot). This sleeving will be colour coded to help you easily identify the left and right, and the line attachment points on the kite are also colour coded to prevent incorrect attachment. Attach the loose ends as instructed using the lark's head knot. You're ready to start unwinding the lines. Unwind them fully as far as the control bar

as described in the kite or wing instruction manual. Do a quick check to make sure they're correctly attached as launching incorrectly with them attached can risk serious injury. Ready? I think you probably are,

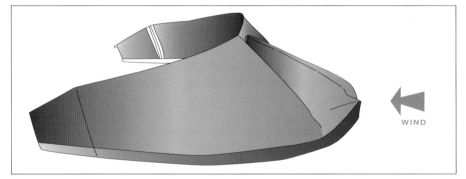

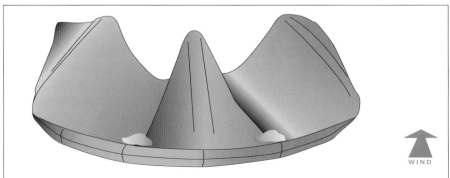

How to launch an inflatable wing

As with the other Flexifoil kites and wings, there are two ways of launching an inflatable wing such as the Storm: assisted launch (recommended for beginners) or solo launch (recommended for more experienced flyers only). The assisted launch is advised because until you're used to the handling there's a chance you could get into difficulties. In big winds and with big wing sizes it's recommended, however much experience you've got, to use the assisted launch. You're going to need to know solo launching so let's take a look at that first.

① For an assisted launch make sure you brief your caddy before you start. There's no difference in the positioning of wing or flyer. The caddy should stand downwind, behind the wing where it's set up on the ground.

② When you're ready to launch, as you start to move backwards and pull gently on the control bar, they hold the downwind tip of the wing up to the wind and, as it lifts up, hold the leading edge of the wing to stabilise it during this phase.

③ With the wing full of wind and ready to go they hold it by the centre of the leading edge from where they can do one of two things: on your launch signal they release the wing, take a few steps backwards to get out of the way, and let you fly the wing to safety; on your signal to abort the launch, grab it quickly, turn it on it's back

▸ *The assisted launch steps 1–3*

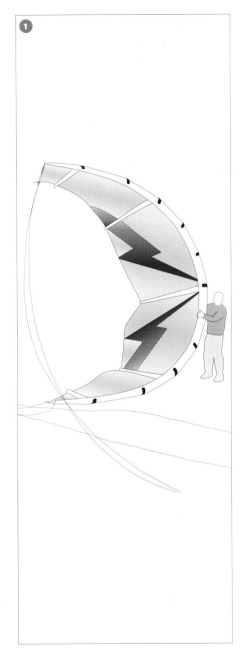

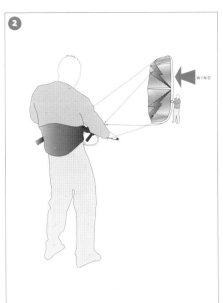

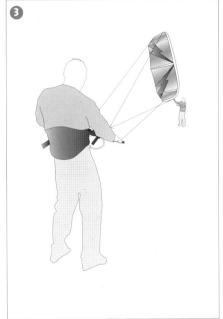

to de-power it and immobilise it again. What you must do is to agree your signals. Flexifoil recommends using hand and arm signals because the noise of wind and water can make it difficult to communicate orally. It's also important for the caddy to simply release the wing at the appropriate moment, not to try and throw it. Once the wing is out of the caddy's hands you follow the normal procedure for steering the wing up to the zenith.

For the unassisted launch let's assume you're in position and so is the wing, on its back at about 45 degrees to window centre, leading edge facing the edge of the wind window.

① Take a couple of paces backwards pulling smoothly, gently and evenly on the control bar. As you do so tension will come onto the downwind tip lines, making the tip rise off the ground. As it does this you will feel pressure beginning to build in the sail.

② Keep moving gently backwards and the downwind tip will rise further. Then tension will come onto the upwind tip and lines, pulling it towards you. As it does so it will unfold and dump its load of sand on the ground. If you don't fold the wing tip over there's a chance the sand won't be removed and it may foul your launch. Hold the bar diagonally in the same plane as the wing to help maintain its position facing the edge of the wind window. You will now feel considerably more pressure on the lines as the wing fills with wind.

▸ *The unassisted launch steps 1–3*

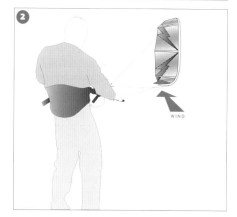

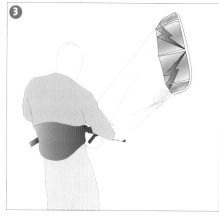

③ Once the wing has got rid of its sand it will lift itself off the ground and as long as you keep even pressure on the flying lines will fly to a safe position to the edge of the wind window.

From here you can steer it up the wind window, pulling gently on the upper tip and lines, until it reaches the zenith, above your head. Neutralise your steering to stabilise the wing there.

Steering the wing

With the wing stable at the zenith, this is the moment when, if this was a kiteboarding session, you would hook in to your harness and get your board leash fastened ready to hit the water. During your first few sessions, while you are mastering the flying controls, you are advised not to hook in. You need to know how to fly the wing confidently before adding new dimensions such as the harness.

At this stage your only way of controlling (as in reducing) power is to move forwards or steer the wing further out of the window. It's going to be a good workout because you'll be dealing with the full power of the wing with your arms, then your body, rather than the other way round. Try moving the wing backwards and forwards across the top of the wind window at first. The steering is very similar to a two-line kite despite the four control lines.

① Pull back gently but firmly on the right side of the control bar, at the same time pushing forward with the left, until you see the wing start to turn to the right. As soon as it's pointing slightly to the right neutralise your steering to let it fly in that direction. It may descend slightly as it does so.

② Before it reaches the edge of the window, pull gently but firmly back on the left end of the control bar until you see the wing turn to face slightly left. Neutralise your steering to let the wing fly back across the top of the window. It will probably rise a little towards centre window and fall again as it moves slightly left. Don't forget, the wind window is curved.

③ Before it reaches the left edge of the window pull back again on the right side and so on. You can stabilise the wing at the zenith by turning the wing to point straight up as you reach window centre.

Once you've done that a few times it's time to try some full loops although that kind of manoeuvrability isn't often called for in kiteboarding.

④ With the wing stable at the zenith, pull back firmly on the right tip of the control bar, pushing forward with the left also. The wing will turn to the right and then continue to turn as long as you keep steering it that way.

⑤ Keep steering it that way and it will turn gradually through 360 degrees, down and to the right, coming round to point straight up the wind window again near window centre. Keep the steering on even when the wing is pointing straight down and accelerating hard. As it comes round towards window centre the pull will be

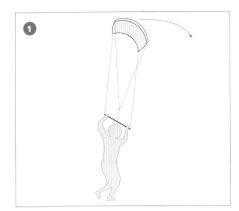

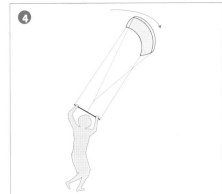

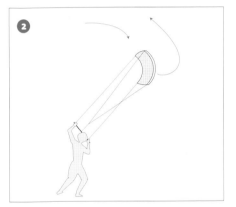

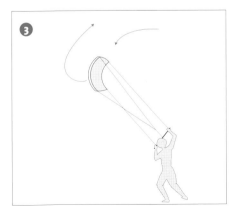

close to max and you will need to lean back, keeping your shoulders well back.

⑥ As the kite comes round full circle and is pointing straight up the wind window neutralise your steering to allow it to climb up towards the zenith. At this point the wing will start to decelerate and lose pull. Just before it reaches the zenith pull back firmly on the left side of the control bar to pull the wing into a left-hand loop. Keep the steering on all the way round until the wing is pointing straight up and climbing up centre window.

Once you have mastered the right and left loop you can fly around and explore the wind window, feeling the pull in different positions in the window. Standing on the ground you will feel good continuous pull doing a flat figure of eight (successive left and right loops) in the sky. Once you get out on the water there's another kind of manoeuvre you will need to know for the occasions when you need to work the wing if the wind is light for the size you're flying. It's a kind of 'S' pattern on its side or sinusoidal that you fly near the edge of the wind window which keeps powering the wing up as you move it around.

⑦ With the wing stable at the zenith, pull back firmly but gently on the right end of your control bar to turn the wing to the right. Keep turning it until it is pointing downwards at 45 degrees. As it comes down the side of the wind window it will begin to power up and accelerate.

⑧ As the wing reaches 45 degrees angle to

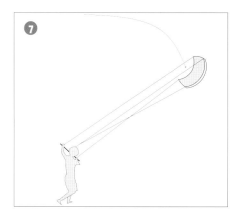

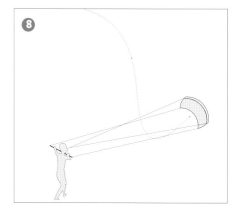

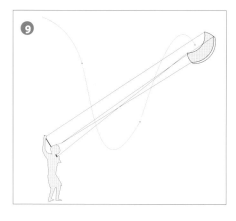

the ground, pull back firmly on the left end of your control bar, turning the wing up at 45 degrees again (a 90 degree turn). Keep the steering on and turn the wing so that it climbs up the wind window.

⑨ Before the wing slows down and loses power pull on the right end of your control bar again to turn the kite through 90 degrees to the right and down again, where it will once again power up and accelerate towards the ground as before.

At this point you can keep the wing moving in a continuous pattern, working it up and down the edge of the wind window to try to gain power. The lower the wing comes in the sky the more lateral pull there will be and the more you can work your board's edges.

Landing an inflatable wing

As with the launch, the landing is a potentially hazardous moment and your landings should always be made with a helper or caddy. It is not possible to solo land and it should not be attempted.

First of all you must have a big enough landing area, away from other site users. If you are in a group of kiteboarders you must agree where your landing and launching area is before starting and always head for when you want to get off your board and land the wing. You need to have your caddy correctly positioned between 25 and 40 metres downwind of you (depending on your line length) at the edge of the wind

Landing an inflatable wing

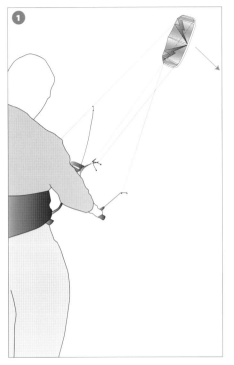

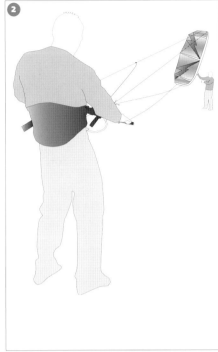

window and they should approach the wing from behind, downwind, as you fly it close to the ground.

① With the wing at the zenith, pull gently on the right end of your control bar and turn the wing to the right. Don't pull it into a full loop; steer it gently but steadily down the edge of the wind window, keeping the leading edge pointing towards the edge of the wind window, never straight down.

As the wing approaches ground level manoeuvre yourself on the ground so

you can fly the wing close to your caddy. Keep flying the wing out towards the edge of the window so there's minimum power.

② Your helper should position themselves so they can approach the kite from downwind, behind it. When your caddy can reach the centre of the leading edge they should grab it, turn the wing on its back and be ready to walk it to a safe position to immobilise it.

You can now detach your board leash and safety leash and walk the wing to a safe position. Place the wing face down, lead-

ing edge pointing into the wind, and weight the leading edge down with sand to immobilise it.

As with the launch the landing should be made when not hooked on to your harness. If you start with the wing at the zenith and fly it down the edge of the window it should have little or no power as it descends.

The de-power system

"The new Storm 2 makes kiteboarding so much easier. The huge de-power range means you don't need so much strength to hold a big kite in a strong wind."

Aaron Hadlow - Flexifoil team kiteboarder

Your Flexifoil Storm II kiteboarding wing is fitted with a highly effective variable power system that is simple to operate. It's all linked to your harness and control bar and, once you start flying hooked into your harness; you will find it very easy to adjust to and wonder how life ever functioned normally beforehand.

Using the de-power system means flying with your harness on so make sure you have fully mastered flying the wing without the harness before you move on to this stage.

On the control bar there are two harness loops or strops in the centre. These are heavy duty vinyl coated loops. The longer one is attached directly to the bar. This is called the power strop and once you hook into this you are committed to full-on power until you unhook again. The other, de-power loop is fitted on to the end of the leader line for the wing's front lines which passes through a special fitting mounted at the centre of the control bar. This is commonly known as the chicken loop, the willy-waggling inference being that if you need to de-power you must be scared (chicken). Further along this leader line towards the line attachments there is a stop fixed in position. Once you are hooked in to the short harness loop, you can regu-late the power by pushing the bar away from you evenly with both hands. With the front lines fixed to your harness this has the effect of pushing the rear lines away, breaking the profile of the trailing edge, changing the angle of attack, spilling some of the wing's wind and losing power.

With skill and practice you will be able to fine-tune the power at various points of your kiteboarding activity, for instance pow-ering-up for jumps, to tweak some extra out of what you're doing. Equally valuably, it enables you to deal with big gusts and squalls out on the water, limiting the power surge and hopefully giving you the breath-ing space you need to ride it out and wait for the power to drop again. In fact, any time you feel that the power is too much and you're hooked into your de-power loop you can use it in this way.

There's a second level of power tuning on the Flexifoil Storm 2 control bar. Between the safety quick release and the line

▶ Right: The de-power system
▶ Far right: The power-up system

HARNESS HOOKED
TO CHICKEN LOOP

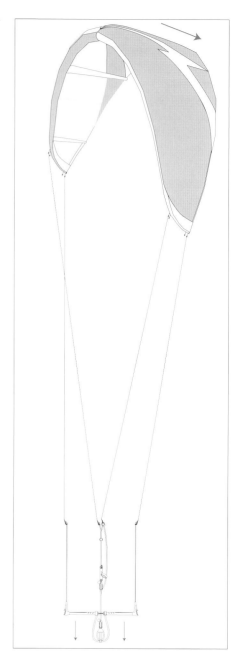

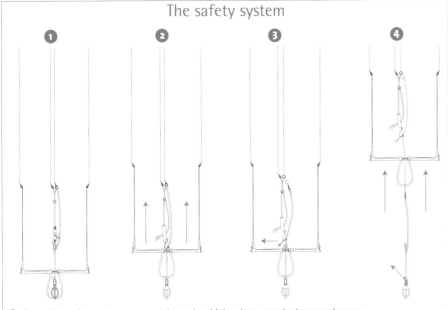

The safety system

① ② ③ ④

① *To use the safety system you must have the chicken loop attached to your harness*
② *Letting go of your bar will cause the kite to de-power.*
③ *Pull the quick release toggle to release the bar and control systems.*
④ *All power will be released from the kite. The control systems will slide along the centre leash.*
    system towards the kite and you may have to pull the safety release on the chicken loop.

line ram air wing on handles or a two-line wing on a control bar you will not have an effective de-power system. In the former scenario you will have the handles to make adjustments to the angle of attack of the wing and, if it all gets too much, a wrist leash for safety (see below). A two-line control bar has either a leash safety system or in some cases is fitted with a third line coming from the centre rear of the wing, attached to the centre of the bar on a leader with a stop. Letting go of the bar pulls on the third line applying maximum brakes and de-powering the wing, causing it to sink to the ground or water.

The safety system

"The safety system on the new Storm II bar is a first, there's no more extra line attached to you but you can kill the power in the kite anytime just by riding through the chicken loop."

Aaron Hadlow – Flexifoil team kiteboarder

attachment point on the centre (front) lines is a tough, anodised clam cleat system which enables you to lock the whole rig at various power settings, varying the range of your de-power. To simplify how it works, if you pull the adjustment toggle towards you it will shorten the front lines, reducing power. Lift and push the adjustment toggle away from you and it will lengthen the front lines or shorten the rear lines accordingly thereby increasing the power setting. Choose your own setting anywhere in between the two extremes.

You can take it a step further too. If you let go of the bar altogether it will slide along the leader line until it meets the stop. This releases the rear lines and keeps the front lines pulled. What normally happens is that the kite almost completely de-powers and flies itself to the edge or top of the wind window where you can recover it. Get plenty of practice on dry land with your de-power system, trying it in every conceivable circumstance, before you find yourself trying to work out how to do it out on the water.

Please be aware that if you're flying a four

Kiteboarding being the dangerous activity that it is, safety very quickly became an issue. Some kind of safety system was needed that would allow you to let go of the control bar or handles to totally de-power the wing but stay attached to it so you could recover it afterwards. Even after the de-power system riders still felt in need of some kind of ultimate, instant get-out, specially for those moments when you're not hooked onto your de-power loop. The Storm I, in

common with its contemporaries, came with exactly this kind of system but as usual it required a leash running from your wrist or harness to one of the (rear) lines. The problem is that for advanced level riders doing jumps and transitions involving full rotations the leash gets in the way, impedes mobility and can foul rider, flying lines or board. With the release of the Storm II control bar Flexifoil took the whole safety quick release principle to a new level, coming up with an advanced safety release system that is totally reliable and enables you to release the kite without the need for a leash!

The safety system is linked to the chicken loop and you'll need to be hooked in to this to be able to make full use of the control bar's safety features. As a first step you can let go completely of the control bar which will slide up to its stop point and de-power the kite. If this is not sufficient, pull the quick release pin toggle located between the control bar and the power-tuning strop on the centre or front lines. At this point the front lines are totally released. This pulls the wing completely out of shape, causing it to lose all power and descend to the ground or water depending on your location. But this isn't a re-ride system, it's for emergency use only. At this point you will no longer be able to consider relaunching as, once actioned, the quick release must be properly reset. You'll need to follow the full 'Back to shore' procedure and reset it on land before you can ride again. As a third level of safety, the

◀ Kiteboarding on the Storm II

bar also has a similar quick release pin on the chicken loop itself. This is your ultimate sanction and might be needed if, for instance, a kite you've already let go to this stage is then snagged by a boat propeller on water or a chair lift on snow. Up to this point you are still attached to the kite and can recover it for the swim back without too much trouble. Actioning this third, ultimate, safety system completely detaches you from the kite and really should only be used in the most extreme of circumstances. You're safely away from trouble but your released kite now represents a danger to other kiteboarders or site users. Now you will have to hope that your kite blows to shore nearby or that someone else helps you recover it in a boat.

It's vitally important that you totally familiarise yourself with all the safety procedures before you go out on a board, including resetting it. The system is only as good as the person operating it and if he hasn't practised... Its even worth trying it in shallow water so you practise recovering your bar and wing in the water before you have to do it for real out of your depth. Remember, your safety system will only work if you are hooked in to your chicken loop. This means you can go for radical, maximum danger moves hooked in.

▸ *Getting ready to go*

Kiteboarding

"Kiteboarding is surely getting easier as the technology advances year on year."

Aaron Hadlow, Flexifoil team kiteboarder

Learning properly from an accredited teacher or school

It goes without saying that what you're about to do is highly dangerous. Not only is there the immense power of the wing, there are the hard edges of the board that can hurt and then there's the small matter of the water, drowning or being lost at sea. In circumstances such as those, as a complete beginner, much the best thing you can do is go and take a series of lessons at an accredited school. That way, you get the right sort of advice and training in a secure environment with rescue boats, full insurance and all the other creature comforts that make learning easier. You can test out equipment before you buy (assuming you haven't already) and see if you actually think you've got the endurance to get through the learning phase. Everybody says that as a complete beginner you've got to expect to drink a lot of water during your first few sessions. But everybody also says that there's nothing like the experience of your first successful getting up on a kiteboard.

Whether you've come from a boarding background or a kiting background, lessons will still be a good idea as there's at least 50% of the package you know little or nothing about at this stage.

Accredited by who exactly? Early on in the life of kiteboarding in the UK, an association was formed with the express purpose of co-ordinating the new sport's activities., especially where that related to safety, teaching and getting new people involved. That organisation is called the BKSA (British Kite Surfing Association) and not only is it the accrediting body for schools, it runs a website and information centre for kiteboarding activities in the UK. Membership costs relatively little (compared with the equipment) and, importantly, includes insurance. You might well find classes available via your local kite or windsurf dealer, at a wind or watersports centre, marina or beach windsurf school. Check that they are BKSA accredited before you book.

There's one worldwide body which has a similar function, instructs instructors, approves courses and issues test standards for equipment. It's called the IKO, the International Kiteboarding Organisation. The IKO is sponsored by a number of big name manufacturers, including Flexifoil, as a means of safely bringing newcomers in and promoting and co-ordinating the development of the sport.

A good kiteboard school will have classes for different skill levels of rider. Be honest about your skill level when choosing your course. Courses are structured to deal with your skill level and progression and like all sports, you need to fully master the basics first and foremost. And check out the site if possible in advance. The best possible conditions for learning are somewhere with plenty of space, flat water and smooth wind but also water that is shallow over a large area. During the learning phase you're going to spend a lot of time falling in the water and restarting. Somewhere with good shallow lagoon water will make the process of getting back in position to restart much, much easier and save you a lot of drinking time, in both senses.

Starting up and riding

"If there's one thing in life you've got to try once, this is it. Kiteboarding is the ultimate sport for me."

Jason Furness, Flexifoil team kiteboarder

Once you've got your kite or wing launched there are two distinct stages to starting up. The first is getting the kite hooked on to your harness and you attached to the board, then taking the whole ensemble to the water. The second stage is actually getting up and riding on the board. This assumes that you're a beginner rider and that you're going to be using a large-volume directional or twin tip for learning and that it's fitted with strap foot bindings. There's a completely different option for anyone who's riding with full foot bindings, because obviously you can't walk to the water when you're strapped on to a board. It means that you've got to set up near the water's edge or just in the water and perform a beach start. And you're going to need a caddy (helper) who can fly the wing while you strap yourself in

▸ *Starting up and riding stages 1–9*

to your bindings and give the control bar to you when you're ready to go. Riding with full foot bindings is an advanced technique, one that you can learn once you've fully mastered the kiteboarding basics.

You're going to need good conditions to help you learn. In kiteboarding terms that means anything from about 8-15 knots of wind speed upwards. Anything more than that and things start to get a bit strong. Anything less and you won't get up on the board. Another factor you must consider is wind direction. Off-shore wind is to be avoided at all costs. Apart from being very lumpy and gusty if it's coming off the land, making everything difficult, it will blow you out to the open sea and maximum danger. Respect the elements and they won't mistreat you. An on-shore wind, whilst almost certainly smooth, will have the tendency to blow you onto the beach as you inevitably travel more downwind at first. The best winds are side-shore, blowing along the beach, or cross-on, blowing diagonally onto the beach. These two allow you, if you're able to successfully tack or reach across the wind, to run out from the beach and back in again, better still getting back upwind. Once you can get back upwind that means you can afford to start trying some jumps, knowing that you can regain all the distance lost downwind in the air during your jump. The better your skill level and the more competent and confident you are, the further you'll be able to go from your start point. You should never, however, under any circumstances ride out of sight of land.

When you're sure that conditions are good and you've made all your preparations, you can start.

Getting on the board for the first time

① Launch the wing on the edge of the wind window and steer it carefully up to the zenith. Now hook in to you harness. This should be on the short loop, the one attached to your safety or de-power system. With this in place you can activate it if you get into difficulties. At this point you should be able to control the wing with one hand, keeping it stable in the minimum power position at the zenith, pushing or pulling on one end of the bar.

② ③ Having established total control over the wing it's time to attend to the other half of the equation, the board. Locate your board and, keeping one hand and one eye on controlling the wing, attach your board leash to your ankle with your free hand.

④ ⑤ ⑥ ⑦ ⑧ Keeping the wing at the zenith, pick up the board with your free hand, tuck it under your arm and make your way carefully to the water, walking far enough out for you and the board to be able to float but not so far that you can't touch the bottom.

So far so good. If your kite skills are good enough you'll be able to get in and out of the water with ease. Practise that sequence until you're completely comfortable with the whole process. What comes next is more dif-

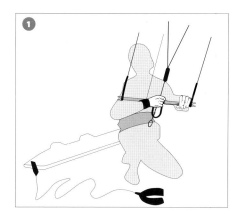

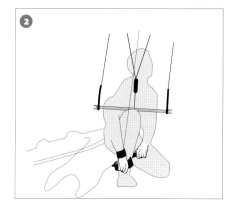

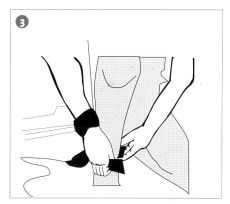

ficult in the sense that now you'll be multi-functioning again, kite and board. But the way equipment is designed now after five years of kiteboarding experience and development, it's all geared towards you succeeding. Be confident, go for it, you'll be amazed how easy it is once you've got it.

⑨ To prepare for your water start you will need to have the board in front and downwind of you. It's easier to move the board than yourself so bring the board in front of you so that you're facing it. Hold the board by its rear strap so it will be easier to manoeuvre.

Water start

See diagrams 1–9 on page 139

① Position the board so it's pointing across the wind and tilt the board at an angle so that you can easily get your feet into the straps. Start with your front or lead foot, then the rear, lying back in the water if necessary. When you put your front foot in, if the wing starts to power up again pull slightly with your front hand and press with the front foot a little to adjust your position rather than overbalancing and having to start all over again.

② This is the most awkward moment, lying on your back, feet in the straps, no power in the wing, and waves washing over your face. Steer the wing across the top of the wind window, to the 'rear' window, opposite to the direction you want to go in. Be careful not to let the wing go too far behind.

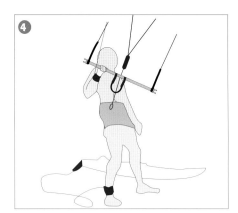

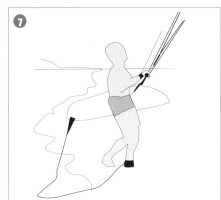

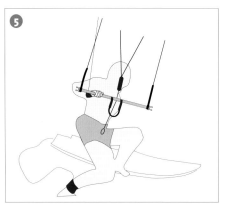

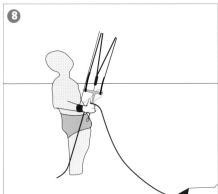

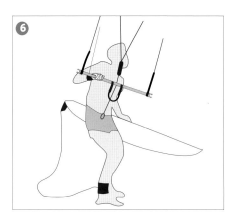

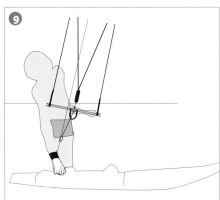

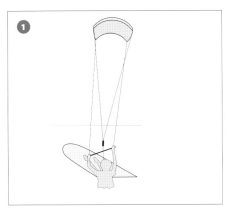

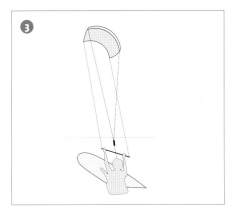

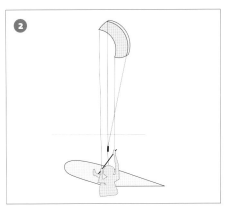

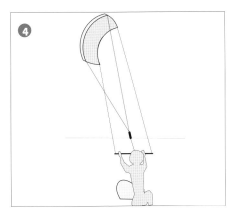

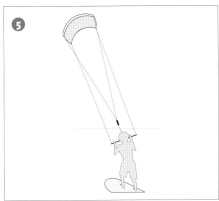

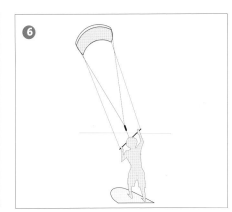

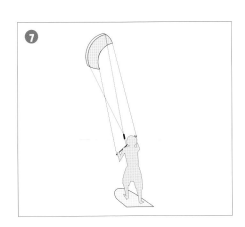

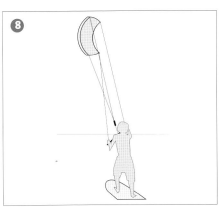

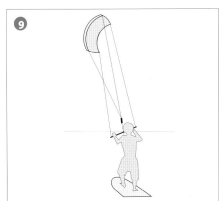

③ ④ ⑤ Now, steer the kite back across the wind window towards the side you want to move towards, bringing the wing down slightly in the window as you do so to power it up. Be careful not to bring the wing too low or it will pull you forwards before you're ready. Keep your knees bent and lean back to lever against the power.

⑥ ⑦ As you feel yourself being pulled forwards, brace your legs to wedge'the flat of the board against the water. Steer the wing up the edge of the wind window. The board will start to slide, pointing slightly downwind to get you going. Keep your legs braced and let the wing pull you gradually up on the board as it climbs the wind window. In lighter winds you may need to use the 'S' pattern to build power up. Strong or light, you will need to press with your rear heel to dig the edge in and aim back upwind. Then press more with your front foot once up and planing to hold your course.

⑧ ⑨ Lock the wing in position on the edge of the wind window. Keep your body flexed and work the board with your feet. It's all in the feet at this stage, a balance of rear foot pressure to work the edge, front foot for course holding.

If all goes according to plan you'll be up on your board and planing, skimming across the surface of the water with the board slightly leaning onto its upwind edge to work against the kite's pull. It may take a few attempts to actually get right.

▶ *Far Right: Beach start 1–2*

There are a couple of things to avoid that will make learning the water start easier: too big a wing size or too much power on your first few attempts, if you haven't yet got used to big power you'll never get up; bringing the wing too low or too far into the wind window will give too much lateral pull and heave you forwards, straight off your board.

Learning the water start is, for obvious reasons, fundamental to all your future activity. You will need to use this technique whenever you fall in the water, once you've relaunched your wing if that has ended up in the water too. Practise water starting to both sides, regular and goofy, so that you're comfortable getting up and planing in either direction.

Beach start

Once you've fully mastered the water start you can think about making your start closer to dry land, what is known as the beach start. If you are fortunate enough to be riding a shallow water lagoon you may not have enough depth for lying down and will need to have this as an alternative. It's much trickier to get right because it all happens quicker but it's a much cooler, cleaner'departure. For this one you need knee depth water at most and to have your board, as before, in front of you, pointing across and slightly downwind. You should be hooked onto your harness on the small harness loop.

• put your wing up at the zenith and put your front foot in its strap.

• get some power back into your wing by bringing it slowly down the wind window. You will feel the power come on and yourself being gradually lifted.

• as the power in the wing lifts you up, swing the wing over towards the side of the wind window you want to move towards, at the same time stepping up onto the board with your rear foot, placing it as close to the strap as you can get it so you get moving quickly.

• keep the wing powered-up and moving towards the edge of the wind window to gain apparent wind and even more power.

• once you're moving forward, stable and powered-up, you can get your rear foot properly into its strap, adjust your body position and dig the back edge in to work the board back upwind slightly.

• with both feet in their straps you can concentrate on planing with the kite locked in position at the edge of the window. It's all in the feet again.

If the wind is strong enough, with a four-line wing such as the Storm II you can virtually lock it in position at 45 degrees to the water and concentrate on steering, holding your line across wind by working the edge, with the board. Apparent wind works again and the more you can steer the board across and slightly upwind the faster you will be able to go. If you want to try and get further upwind, with the water to lever against you you, can bring the kite or wing further down the wind window to power up and use heel pressure to carve the edge into the water, wedging the board and pointing it more

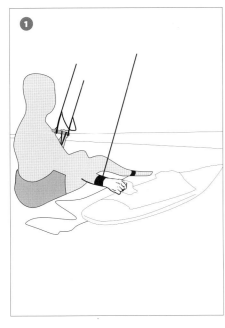

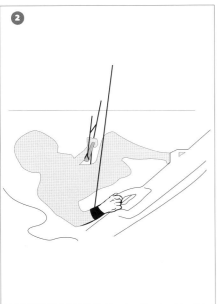

upwind. Once you're pointing the right way take the wing back up the edge of the window and press with the front foot on the board to straighten up again.

If the wind is on the light side for your size of wing or kite, you will need to work it more using the S pattern. The effect of this on the board is that as the wing descends towards the bottom of the S it picks up power, accelerating towards the edge of the window. The rider must work the backside edge and steer upwind to avoid catching up with the wing, causing it to lose power and possibly collapse. The wing will gradually lose power as it climbs back towards the top of its S before the cycle begins again. You need to find a good rhythm of powering up, increasing speed, turning upwind and then gradually straightening again as the wing / kite climbs. The weaker the wind the more exaggerated the S of the kite and weave pattern of the board.

Of course you could use a big 'floaty' board in light wind but riders are generally happier waiting on the beach for the wind to build up so they can get out and go bonkers massively powered-up on their tiny trick boards. There are even people who've succeeded in stacking two LEI kites together, giving a total sail area of over 25 m², and being able to get upwind in as little as 5 knots because of it. Old habits die hard it seems; I wouldn't mind betting the person who thought of that started off their power kiting career flying Flexifoil power kites.

Changing direction and turning round

"Learning any skill is worthwhile as it will help you with something more complicated later on. Gybing is an outdated concept in kiteboarding now but the skills learned will benefit wave and frontside riding later. Even on flat water it's really good fun doing a hard carve gybe on a twin tip or wakeboard and popping the board back round on the exit."

Chris Calthrop, Flexifoil team kiteboarder

We're talking about that well-known spelling conundrum, gybing. If you're using a directional board it's an essential. Even for those of you riding twin tips it's still a cool manoeuvre you can use and that is useful to know. Riding a wakeboard with full foot or ankle bindings or twin tip means that gybing presents a different set of issues as it will leave you riding backside on the frontside edge, that's to say, leaning forward rather than back and flying the wing over your leading shoulder. What we're interested in is the standard directional gybe and the frontside twin tip alternative that is in fact an advanced manoeuvre; don't be disappointed if you don't get it straight away

In one sense the directional gybe is similar to the basic windsurfing gybe which brings the rider round to ride on the other opposite edge of the board from the one they were on before gybing. But there all similarity ends

as, with no fixed mast to hold onto, it becomes a question of balance and timing to turn the board, step over into the foot straps on the other side and resume planing, all the while balancing yourself against the pull of the kite. There's a potentially scary moment when you're out of the straps and face on to the wing and timing is very much the crucial factor. You are strongly advised to try the foot movements several times on your board on dry land, without the wing, so you are confident about that element before you try it on water. No tricky foot movements needed on your twin tip, making it in principle easier, but with the added technicality of a big shift of body weight and a body position leaning forwards as opposed to the more natural backwards lean.

① You're planing along with good forward speed. The board is flat rather than riding on the edge. Time to unhook from your harness and get ready to move. There is no need to unhook on your twin tip!

② Take your rear foot out of its foot strap and put it just in front of the strap. Flex and press with your front foot to tilt the board forwards more, pressing the rail into the water. Bend your rear knee at the same time to make the tilting smooth, firm and even. Twin tip riders initiate the turn by pressing more with their front foot toes to bring the board flat, body position more upright.

③ Control the tilt of the board with your free (rear) foot. Steer the wing straight up to the zenith where it will stay during the next phase. Hold the control bar or handles

at arm's length and start to physically turn the board with your feet. Twin tip riders can shift their weight forwards more and start using toe side pressure to turn the board ready to power the wing up again quickly; directional riders still have one crucial phase to complete as described in the next three steps,

④ As the board turns you find your body coming round to ride backside, back towards the wing. Keep the wing at the zenith. Now take your front foot out of its strap and bring your rear foot up so that you're standing, feet parallel and pointing forwards along the board, just beside or behind the front foot strap.

Keeping the wing at the zenith still, quickly reverse the positions of your feet, putting what was your rear foot into the front strap and your other foot into the rear strap. Whichever way you got to this point you will now need to power the wing up again quickly to drive through the final part of the turn and be able to work the edge and hit that return reach.

⑤ Before you've got the board through its turn, start the wing moving again downwards into the power zone and towards the edge of the wind window that you now want to move towards for your return run. You'll have lost speed through the turn and powering-up again quickly will help prevent the board wallowing. Lean back over your heels or forwards over your toes to counteract the pull and off you go again in the opposite direction.

If you can master the gybe then in many

ways you've got over the most difficult bit. The things to avoid if you want to have the best chance of hitting a good gybe are not having enough forward speed going into the manoeuvre, not tilting the board enough, allowing power back into your wing too soon resulting in wipe out and not getting your wing going soon enough to power up again, resulting in sinking. It's a lot to think about and again may take you many attempts to get right. To make it easier, try it all on a big volume board with a wing that is not too powerful. The idea is to make it one continuous and smooth movement, turning the board quickly and getting it moving again before it has a chance to slow and sink.

The chances are that in fact you'll be learning on a twin tip board in which case there's no gybe needed. That was very much the reason they were created, firstly to eliminate the tricky stage of gybing as a hindrance to progress (lesson learned from windsurfing), secondly to facilitate an altogether trickier (as in range and variety of tricks) style of riding for people who progressed beyond the basic level. But you still need to know how to turn round. In fact we described almost the identical sequence in the kite landboard chapter earlier in the book, those being twin tips too. It's a logical process of manoeuvres with the kite and board, the object being over time to learn to change or reverse direction without coming to a complete stop, keeping yourself powered up and moving. One step at a time:

• as you're planing along, steer the wing up the edge to top centre window where it

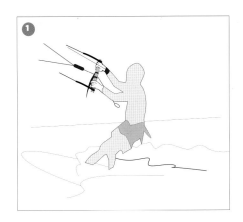

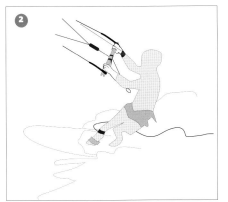

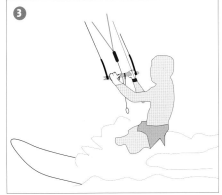

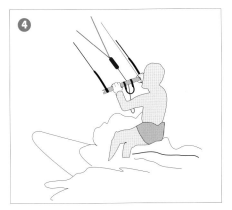

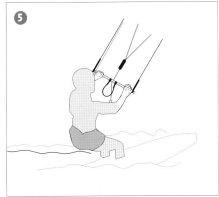

◀ Changing direction 1–5

will lose power and you will slow down.

- as you slow down almost to a stop, shift your weight towards the centre of the board in a more upright body position, ready to go back the other way.
- before you feel the board sink steer the wing towards the edge you want to move towards, bringing the kite lower in the window and bracing your body for the power coming back on.
- lock the wing in position, lean back, find your balance and pressure points and away you go leading with your other foot.

If you can start up, plane on the board, work the edges to go upwind a bit more and turn round to get back to your start point you've got all the basic manoeuvres you need to start out in the exciting world of kiteboarding, the most exhilarating new extreme sport around. Now it's practise, practise, practise. It's good to go solo riding but you will learn a lot by riding with other, more experienced riders, watching what they do, asking them how they do it. With your own growing level of skill and experience and the benefit of theirs you will progress quicker and soon be ready for some more radical and dangerous moves.

Stopping

With luck you're only going to need to stop for one reason, when you want to get back onto dry land, but it may be that other emergencies dictate that you stop out on the water. A dead stop will sink you for sure. Even on a larger volume directional board

the chances are you will be down in the water although your wing should be safely positioned and you shouldn't need to water launch it. You should be hooked on to your short harness loop or de-power system.

- as you are reaching across the wind and are nearing the beach, start steering the wing up the edge of the wind window to lose power and slow down.
- at the same time start leaning back to work the rear edge and turn your board upwind.
- steer the wing to the zenith, and when the board is pointing upwind press with your front foot to bring the board and yourself upright.
- step off the board quickly and, keeping the wing stable at the zenith with one hand, pick up your board with the other and leave the water, detach yourself from the board and follow the normal procedure for an assisted landing.

The idea is to stop close enough to dry land to be in shallow water and step off the board. If you have to execute your stop in deeper water obviously you won't have that luxury. But your wing should be stable up at the zenith and it will be another chance to practise your water restart. It's all a question of timing, as usual. With skill and practice you'll be able to stop suddenly, but always be careful as you steer the wing up the window not to get it too far behind you or it will pull you over, or too powered up or you'll be heading for an unexpected jump. Stopping at exactly the right place on the edge of the beach is an acquired skill.

Jumping

"You need good wind, a fast efficient kite, a thin board.... and balls. Send it!"

Chris Calthrop, Flexifoil team kiteboarder

It's one thing checking out the great photos in kiteboarding magazines and books such as this, checking out what the pros are up to on the latest videos and DVDs, but it's quite another actually witnessing a skilful rider (better still a big competition) hitting some big airs. As soon as you see it you know you want to give it a go. It's sick, it's cool, it's totally impressive and the hang time seems to go on for ever. With variable incidence power control a rider can even turn the power level up while in the air to extend a jump. With tricks besides. Watching the likes of Hadlow, Furness, Calthrop, Seales, Wharry, Trow and Co. flying past, ten metres above the water, upside down, is a huge attention grabber and is one of the main reasons so many people want to learn the sport.

There are three distinct phases to each jump: preparation and getting air born, being in the air and the landing. It may take longer to learn the final element and you must be prepared once again for a lot of falls and water drinking, having just learned how to ride well enough not to. No gair. ithout pain. Even when you've learned how to do the whole thing it won't stop there because once you prove to yourself that you can do it, you'll want to keep going for bigger, better, more complicated jumps. And that generally means big wipe-outs. At least as a kiteboarder you've got the cushioning water to land in rather than a hard surface to slam into. Nevertheless, be careful, that water can still seem very hard and hurt a great deal if you hit it at speed.

For your first attempts it will be better if you're on flat water rather than waves or a swell. Learn how to jump properly first, then you can start playing trampolines with the water contours later on. As ever you'll be wanting a smooth wind, strong enough to get you off the water but not so much that everything happens too fast or too hard. Try with a medium-size kite while you get used to the mechanics, technique and sensations. Remember, this is pretty much maxi danger: in the air, over water, powered by a big kite wing and not in 100% control of what happens next, however good you are. It's better to be hooked on to the short harness loop or de-power system during your first jumps. It allows you to control the power before and during the jump and makes it simple to let go of everything if you get into difficulties in mid jump. Fixed in to the long loop you can't control it and will therefore have maximum power all through the jump. If you're riding with a two-line wing you should unhook altogether for exactly that same safety reason.

Jumping almost always moves you some distance downwind during the time that you're in the air, the bigger the jump, the greater the downwind travel. Be ready for this, make sure you've got a clear zone at least three kite-line lengths downwind before you start your attempts. That means clear of other riders and water users but also clear of rocks, moored boats, the beach

itself, piers, jetties, anything that can pose a potential risk. For a cool jump you need a combination of board speed and good timing:

- steer the wing low down (30 degrees) on the edge of the wind window so that you're as powered-up as possible and sailing slightly upwind, pressing hard with your heels to work the edge in the water. You need a good body position to get ready to go air born, knees bent, body flexed and braced, ready to spring.
- keep working the edge so as not to lose any speed. Start steering the wing so that it comes slightly back into the wind window, pulling very slightly with the line attached to the top wing tip.
- as you do this try to relax some of the pressure on the board so you are less on the edge and more on the flat of the board. Keep moving the wing towards centre top of the wind window, pointing straight up.
- keep working on the board until the pull of the wing in centre window is too much to hold. Now, spring into the air letting the wing pull you off the water as you do so. The wing should still be in centre window.
- all being well, you are now air born and will really feel the lift effect of the wing. Enjoy every second but keep a careful eye on the wing and make sure it stays where you put it. Don't get it moving towards the edge again too early or you'll have a very hard fast splashdown; keep it as directly above your head as possible.
- get back into a good braced, flexed body shape for the landing, which is coming up quickly. The wing may well be a little

behind you now and it's time to get it back into meaningful action. Don't let it go too far behind you. Pull slightly on your forward hand to start bringing it forwards in the window and have a look to make sure it has started turning. Getting power back in the wing at the right moment means a softer landing, too much means a hard, fast landing.

- brace yourself for splashdown. Watch the water as you approach to really spot that landing and if you think you're going too fast with the wing pulling more than you'd like, try and place the board so it's pointing slightly downwind to lose a bit of speed. If the opposite happens and you land heavily with little power, dig your rear edge in, steer the board as upwind as possible to try and power the wing up quickly by bringing it low in the window then powering upwards to lift yourself up and get moving again. Bend your knees on landing to absorb any impact and get yourself planing again quickly.

The trick with learning to jump is having the correct wing size up: too big and you won't be able to manoeuvre it quickly enough, too small and it will be too fast. When you get it right and you start nailing the whole jump you really are on the way to max-ing your sensations. If it's that good to watch, imagine what it must feel like up there on the board.

But don't stop there. You can learn how to control the power of your jumps to go higher or lower, master your wing control to get the best possible landings and go for bigger and better jumps. Then you start throwing in

some tricks, starting with some basic grabs perhaps, and then see where you go after that. It won't be too long I'm sure before you're hitting those big upside down numbers, some rotations perhaps.

Water re-start

"It's not easy but you soon learn it or you swim."

Jason Furness, Flexifoil team kiteboarder

As if it hasn't been mentioned enough already, don't forget you're going to do a lot of falling off your board while you learn how its done and indeed afterwards if you start progressing on to big jumps and tricks. So it's imperative that you know how to water re-start. In fact kiteboarders rarely go more than a few hundred metres offshore so swimming back in is no great issue. It is very tiring but since you'll have to dry out your wing before you start again you'll have a bit of recovery time once you're back on dry land.

There's a strong argument that using an inflatable wing makes you lazy and doesn't place enough emphasis on learning to keep it in the air even during crashes. Certainly the idea is that once you progress beyond learner status the water relaunch shouldn't be needed anywhere near as much. A lot, clearly, is going to depend on what type of wing and what line set-up you're using. If

▶ *Water restart steps 1– 4*

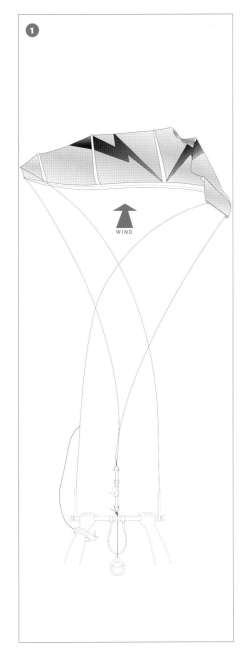

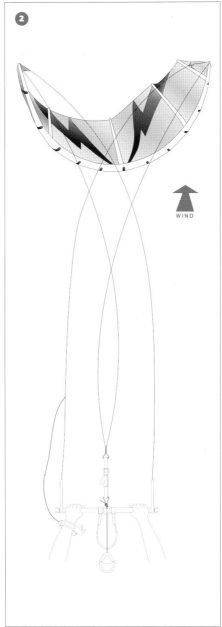

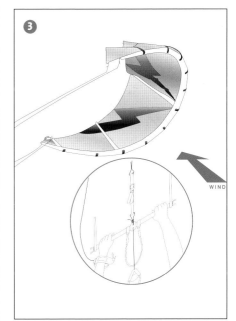

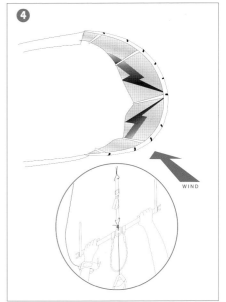

you're using a ram air wing such as a Blade, already your chances of successfully re-launching are about 50/50 at best. And if you're using a two-line set up to fly your ram air wing you're almost certainly looking at a swim back unless you're very lucky and very quick. The problem being that as soon as water gets inside the wing through the vents, it becomes virtually impossible to re-launch. That goes for four-line riders too. But at least they have a chance to either reverse launch or launch in the normal way, depending on how the wing has landed.

When you end up in the water it may be as a result of a big wipe-out during which you've let go of your wing and come off your board so the first stage is to recover your equipment. If it was a big wipe-out you might well be winded and need a few seconds to get your breath and bearings back. It's going to be hard work to relaunch, especially if there are waves and you keep getting a face full of water. The wing may have landed in any kind of position: leading edge up, leading edge down, on its back, face towards you. face down or away, or in a complete heap because you activated your safety system. To restart in water:

- the first thing to check once you've got your bearings is how the wing has landed.
- recover your control bar or handles using the leash if you've let go of them and make sure the lines are not snagged round your legs or anything else that could affect re-launch.
- check where your board is, not too far away if you've got your leash properly attached.

The wing will normally drift downwind of you on the water.

- if your ram air four-line wing has landed leading edge up you should have little problem launching it in the normal way, unless it then falls face down on the water. With the bridles submerged under the wing you're done for.
- during a standard relaunch you may need to swim backwards to help get enough tension on the lines to lift the wing off but, once launched, it will power up quickly, especially if it has drifted near centre window.
- quickly steer the wing to a safe position at the edge or zenith of the wind window so you can get ready for your water start.

It's quite common for the wing to land leading edge down. If you're using a four-line set up you can try to reverse launch the wing in the normal way. Again, if the wing falls face down at this point you're in for a swim. If it falls on its back a quick pull on the rear lines should get it upright again, on its leading edge. Then:

- pull back on the bottom of the handles to put tension on the rear lines. You may need to try and swim backwards as you do this until there is sufficient tension for the wing to develop enough lift to start reversing. Pull back equally on both sides.
- as the wing lifts off backwards and reaches a height above the water where you are sure you can turn it, pivot one handle so the rear line is pushed forwards and the front line has tension on it.

The wing should turn around its centre point until the leading edge is pointing straight up. Pivot the other handle so that both front lines are pulled to move the wing up the window away from danger. Steer it to a safe position at the zenith where you can get ready for your water start.

In both cases, if the wing is directly downwind of you it may be a good idea to reorientate it closer to one edge so as to avoid full and unexpected power up at the moment of take off. This can be done by either swimming to one side or by pulling on one handle only to move the wing across before you relaunch.

It's quite different water launching an inflatable wing such as the Storm. Even so it's certainly no cakewalk and just because you've bought an inflatable wing doesn't mean it does it all automatically. There's still lots to learn and you've got to get it right. There's a dead position from which there's no recovery no matter how much you spend on equipment and courses. If the wing is down on its face, leading edge down in the water so you can see the back of the wing, then no amount of water relaunchability is going to help.

From any other position down on the water, something in the Storm's favour straight away is its less extreme aspect ratio in relation to some other competition standard inflatable wings, which are enormously elongated and more difficult to manoeuvre into a relaunch position. One factor with inflatable wings is that they can occasionally relaunch themselves when you're not expecting it so watch out for that first and foremost. Technically, it's feasible to reverse the wing off the water but in reality this is extremely difficult when you're in water that is out of your depth.

If the wing has come down on its trailing edge then it's a simple job to relaunch by pulling back on the control bar. Be aware of the wing's position in the wind window, however. Too much power could be a problem so try to get offwind by swimming to one side or by pulling on one side of the control bar only at first, to move it towards the edge before you attempt the relaunch.

Likewise if the wing is down on one side or wing tip. You will need to steer the wing to one edge (the one that the leading edge is facing) first. Then:

- pull back on the side of the control bar attached to the upper tip and swim in the opposite direction from which you are steering the wing at the same time.
- when the wing nears the edge of the window you can pull on the lines attached to the upper tip only to lift the wing off the water.
- then steer the wing carefully up the edge of the wind window to the zenith.

The tricky one is if your wing comes down leading edge down, face towards you. At this point you have to try and get the kite to fall over on its back but this is easier said than done. If there's a good wind blowing the wing will keep powering up and pulling you downwind. The Storm II has been designed with easy water relaunch in mind and is relatively easy to get onto one tip. Nevertheless you must try and de-power the wing by swimming towards it and taking tension off the flying lines:

- swim towards the wing until tension goes from the flying lines. At this point the wing will fall onto its back. Be aware of where your flying lines are so as not to get them snagged on you or your board.
- pull on one side of your control bar to bring the wing up onto one tip or side. This may require swimming backwards a little to get tension on that side.
- once the wing is on one tip, steer it to the side you have chosen and don't change your mind, this will simply prolong the whole process. Pull back on the lines attached to the upper tip. The wing may move slowly so be patient.
- once the wing reaches the edge of the wind window, a further pull on the lines attached to the upper tip will lift the wing off the water.
- steer the wing carefully up the edge of wind window to the zenith and get ready for your water start.

Whichever type of wing you're using, water re-launch is a relatively advanced technique so you may not master it straight away. A very good idea is to practise in shallow water near the shore until you're confident you can get a good percentage (50% or more). That way you'll be ready when it does happen half a mile off shore and won't be so daunted by the prospect.

With your wing back up at the zenith it's time to get up on your board again using

your water start. You've already done the hardest part, which is to recover your wing and, if all goes according to plan, you'll quickly be up and planing again. You may not be so fortunate and so the final part of your basic kiteboard training is what do to do if it all goes horribly wrong.

Back to shore

It's going to happen sooner rather than later. As usual, there's a simple step by step procedure, one that you definitely need to practise several times in shallow water before it happens in choppy sea further out than you care to imagine. In those circumstances, if there's no rescue boat around, it becomes not so much a question of getting started again as saving your life. Your board will be on the end of its leash and will be very useful presently for getting everything back to land. For now you need to concentrate on finding your control bar or handles and making sure the flying lines aren't twisted around your legs or the board under the water.

Once you've found the control bar or handles start winding in the flying lines while swimming slowly towards the wing. Wind as far as just in front of the wing.

Now straighten out the wing. If it's an inflatable the first thing to do is deflate the vertical battens using the valves, starting with the tips and working your way inwards to the centre one last. Then deflate the leading edge. Each time you deflate a tube be careful not to allow any water into the tubes. Likewise, once they're deflated, close the valves properly.

From this point the procedure is the same for ram air or inflatable. Place the control bar on one tip and roll the wing up around the control bar. If rolling up a ram air try to squeeze the air out through the vents as you roll to make a less bulky package.

With the kite wing rolled you can put it on your board. Take your harness off so the hook doesn't cause discomfort while lying on the board, attach it to the rear strap, lie on the board and paddle back in.

Once you're back to dry land it's time to re-inflate those tubes or dry out your ram air and a quick check that the flying lines are OK before getting yourself relaunched and re-started. It's possible to buy a kiteboarding back pack or waist pouch to wear while you're riding. Either of these would be a useful accessory to have during this exercise because you can put the wing in the pouch or pack, attach the harness to it and it to your rear foot strap and paddle your board in towing the whole lot behind you. You can practise all this on those days when there's enough wind to fly the wing but not to get up on the board. Make sure it's second nature to you before the issue is forced on you in less forgiving circumstances.

Basic rules for kite-boarding safety

As mentioned, when you start playing around with the awesome power of traction wings and then add the extra mystery ingredient of water it's a recipe for extreme fun but also for extreme danger. Safety first, sec-

ond and third is very much the order of the day because if it ever appears that kite-boarding is unnecessarily risky there will be calls for it to be prohibited. Safety was the primary reason for the founding of the BKSA (British Kite Surfing Association) who quickly took on the role of educating riders and training trainers as soon as the new sport started getting attention and attracting newcomers. They have drawn up a set of basic safety guidelines, which apply to riders of all skill levels but especially to beginner riders. They identify a number of basic skills a rider must have acquired in order to move successfully onto the water. With thanks to the BKSA, those guidelines are reprinted here in full.

Kite surfing is an extreme sport and is therefore potentially dangerous to both the kite surfer and others. The over-riding need is for rider responsibility. It shouldn't put anybody off or sound too officious but with so many newcomers to kite surfing it was felt necessary to lay out a complete set of safety guidelines.

Kiteboarding or boarding should not be attempted without appropriate instruction.

The minimum competence levels are considered to be :

Level 1: Kite Flying Skills

- understand all aspects of safe handling of kites on land and water.
- be able to launch and land (unaided) on a specified spot on land.

Level 2: Basic Water Skills

- body surfing with kite (along and back to shore).
- water launching onto board.

Level 3: Basic Kite Surfing Skills

- getting on a board and travelling a distance under kite power.
- performing emergency stop on water – getting off the board quickly and stopping with the kite aloft.
- returning to base on land either by kiteboarding, paddling or body surfing home.

General safety guidelines

- stay clear of power lines and overhead obstructions.
- never fly a kite in a thunderstorm.
- always inform the beach warden, life-guard or coast guard of where and when you will be kiteboarding (kites hitting the water can look like planes crashing to the uninitiated). Britain's beaches, airspace and ocean environment belong to everyone and must be kept safe, clean and free.

Kite contra-indications:

- if you cannot walk backwards when the kite is flying at minimum power (overhead) the kite is too big or the wind is too strong.
- never tether yourself to the kite with a closed system. Only use open quick-release harness systems, if any.

Never attempt kiteboarding if you don't have a good level of kite flying experience.

Site etiquette:

- do not lay kite lines across anyone's path.
- do not launch or land in crowded areas.
- always announce you are launching a kite.
- select a safe launching site.
- prevent kites from relaunching by weighting them down with sand or other ballast.
- disable unattended kites.

Water:

- never kite surf in areas congested with swimmers, boats, other craft and obstacles.
- never go out on the water without telling another person where you're going.
- always maintain a downwind safety buffer zone to allow for being pulled downwind.
- a kiteboarder must know the rules of the sea including navigation laws and abide by them at all times.
- instruction must be taken from an experienced kiteboarder before attempting kiteboarding for the first time.
- a kiteboarder should be fit and healthy and over 18 years of age (under 18s must provide a written parental permission).
- if going offshore, kiteboard in pairs or with a rescue boat in attendance.
- never kiteboard in conditions which are too extreme for you or your equipment.

Equipment:

- all manufacturers' instructions and safety guidelines must be read and followed with particular regard to the limitations of the product.

- equipment must be checked regularly for wear and tear and repaired or replaced before going onto the water.
- always use adequate safety equipment.
- be safe – wear a helmet.

Other essential equipment

The full list of kiteboarding essentials depends to a large extent on where you're going to do the majority of your riding. The air and water temperature will make a huge difference, for example, to the thickness of your wetsuit, and indeed whether you wear one at all. But suffice to say there's an armoury of other pieces of equipment aside from the board and wing that you'll need to have before you can get out on the water, wherever you're planning to plane.

Harness: Absolutely essential. Generally available in two styles: the belt harness and the seat harness. The former fits around the waist and the other has a full crotch fit. The seat version helps get the centre of pull and balance much lower making boarding more stable.

Wetsuit: Absolutely essential. Available in different thicknesses (anywhere from 3 to 7mm) depending on how cold it's likely to be, 3 to 5 being the most common. Also in different leg and arm lengths with a shorty suit in 3mm being the kind of thing for warm water riding. Even in tropical waters, if you plan to ride all day a shorty suit can protect you from crash landings and hypothermia. Different men's and women's fits. Always try on in the shop before you buy. If they won't let you, go somewhere else.

Flotation and buoyancy: Absolutely essential. Some belt style harnesses now incorporate buoyancy.

Crash helmet: Absolutely essential. There's no excuse for not wearing one.

Board leash: Attaches the board to your ankle or rear of your harness via a Velcro strap fastening and length (2 metres approx.) of vinyl cord. You can ride without one if you like but you're going to be chasing your board all over the place.

Safety system: Absolutely essential. Comes as standard with most wings nowadays.

Large ground stake: For keeping wings of varying sizes ready but immobilised on days of varying wind.

Wind meter: Expect to pay handsomely for any hand-held meter with any accuracy.

Puncture repair kit: Absolutely essential. Like a bicycle puncture repair kit but for the inflatable tubes that are vital to your wing's functioning.

Basic human repair kit: Plasters, antiseptic, bandages, sling, this is an extreme sport remember? .

Sun cream and ultra violet protection: Yes, even in northern Europe. For those parts of you not covered by your suit and which will be exposed to the elements all day.

Sunglasses: As above but for your eyes.

That's what you need to get you going. What about all those things that can happen during the day that you need to cover yourself for? The more you kiteboard the more gear you're going to accumulate for doing different things and the more potential for hardware failure to spoil your day out. Remember:

- spare flying line sets in case of a damaged or broken line.
- spare control bar.
- splicing and sleeving kit for making adjustments or repairs to flying lines.
- spare fins for your board.
- spare straps or bindings.
- tool kit with spare fittings for fins and bindings.
- spare harness (an old one perhaps).
- different types of board depending on the conditions, a larger volume directional or twin tip for light winds and a wake or mini board for strong winds and flat water.
- a reserve supply of energy bars and drinks in case, as can easily happen, you stay out riding a long time and need to get emergency energy in your body once you're back on dry land.
- a waterproof watch so you can actually keep track of time instead of losing it.

Having dealt with all the important and essential items, it's worth pointing out that kiteboarding, in common with other board and surf sports, is a very style conscious affair. Clothing manufacturers sponsor the riders up to the eyeballs, fuelling the whole thing even further. Sure, there's looking cool during the après-surf once the water action's finished, but there's a great deal of sartorial splendour out there on the water too. Large numbers of riders seem to resent the anonymity of the standard dark neoprene wetsuit and you'll find that there are thousands of garments on the rails and shelves to choose from now that will cover your modesty if that's what you want.

The Storm II components

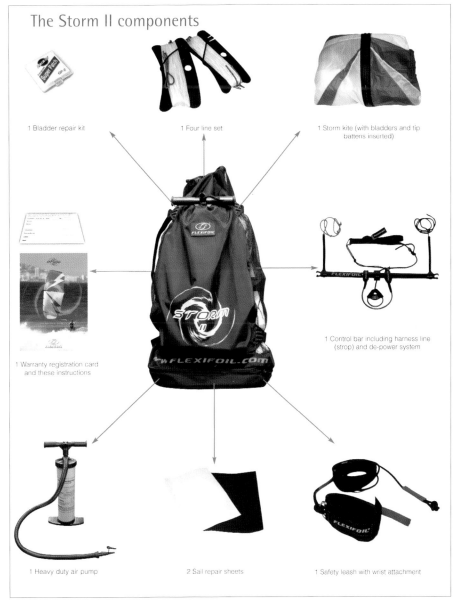

1 Bladder repair kit

1 Four line set

1 Storm kite (with bladders and tip battens inserted)

1 Warranty registration card and these instructions

1 Control bar including harness line (strop) and de-power system

1 Heavy duty air pump

2 Sail repair sheets

1 Safety leash with wrist attachment

Body surfing or dragging

It's good fun, you don't need a board or buggy but you will need a wetsuit because dragging your body along through shallow water is just inviting those rocks, razor shells and other flotsam and jetsam to enter where they're not at all welcome. It's also a good way of getting used to flying and working the kites and wings while in the water and anyone signing up for a beginner kiteboarding course can expect to learn to body surf as part of their basic training.

Any stack of kites or single big kite or wing will do the job and any line configuration, two or four. It's not complicated to do, in fact it's much like skidding on land. It's not too technical to get yourself going and the main thing to avoid is getting yourself out of your depth of water until you're confident of not dumping the kites in the water while body dragging. You'll need some kind of flotation jacket to help make sure your body is well up in the water if the kites or wing de-powers for any reason. If you're a harness user you can use that as long as you've got a de-power, safety and or quick-release system ready in case you hit a problem.

If you were paying attention earlier on you'll know all about flying a flat figure of eight pattern with your wing or kite slightly above mid window as a means of generating constant pull on dry land. That's what you do to start skidding on the ground and, whereas you lean backwards for a good skid, you're now going to be lying on your front, letting the kites pull you along and keep your head out of the water at the same time. Start by standing up and once the power comes on you plunge forward onto your front, keeping your arms free for steering the kite or wing. The more consistently you can keep the power on the less water you're going to drink.

Be aware that body surfing and dragging is not something you can or should do reaching across the wind. It's one direction only, downwind. That means you can only really use a sideshore wind to go along the shoreline, never getting too far from land and being able to leave the water to get back upwind when you need. Avoid offshore winds as these obviously could drag you out to the danger of the open sea. It's perfectly possible to cross rivers, lakes and reservoirs depending on their size but you need to be sure you have the skill and strength to get across. And some means of getting back again afterwards with your gear.

Care of
the **kite**

THE MORE POWER KITING that you do the more equipment you're going to accumulate and the more serious and potentially dangerous its purpose often becomes. The object is to enjoy the danger while minimising the risk, both to yourselves and others. And then there are the kites and wings themselves and the flying lines that control them. It can all potentially either endanger or save your life and needs to be looked after and maintained accordingly. Apart from anything else, you've quite possibly spent a good deal of your hard-earned money buying them. And who knows, one day you might even want to start selling some of it secondhand, in which case, the better the condition it's in the more you'll get for it.

Nothing deteriorates ripstop nylon sail cloth and other fabrics quite as efficiently as ultra violet light from the sun. Unless it's salt water. And sand. Or the three together. So, whilst beach sites are great for wind and space, they're also a potential hazard for your kites.

Yes it's a good idea to have different kites ready to use in case of changing wind but bear in mind that a kite that's left out all day in bright sunlight will quickly fade and deteriorate.

If your kite gets wet with salt water you should rinse the fabric when you get it home. Use warm (not hot), mildly soapy water, wash by hand, then rinse and dry everything thoroughly before finally packing

◀ *Keep your gauze clean for better flying*
▶ *Shake out all the sand when flying on beaches*

it away. In fact any kite that is packed away wet from sea or rain on the flying site must be completely dried out at home. Be careful too of tar and oil on beach sites as these are very difficult to remove from nylon sailcloth.

Empty sand out from ram air kites as it will damage the fabric and interfere with flying. Check your kites over regularly, specially for signs of strain around the bridle or flying line attachment points and any damage to the bridle itself. Small tears and holes can be mended with clear adhesive repair tape available from your dealer. Bigger tears or holes or other general repairs should be returned to Flexifoil, either directly or through your dealer.

Even with regular heavy use, every weekend, a kite should last you two or three years if looked after properly. After that time it may well be generally used and stretched, specially if used extensively at or above its wind range limit, to an extent that replacement is the only option. It will certainly never fly again as new.

On an inflatable wing you should check over your inflatable tubes regularly. Punctures can be easily repaired in a similar way to a bicycle repair. You may need to put the inflated tube in a bowl of water to identify the leak before effecting a repair. Check the leading edge for signs of scuffing or small nicks and tears and the line attachment points to make sure they are secure. And there's a big stress point where the leading edge is joined to the sail. Check along the length of this join.

▸ Top: Repairing a kite
▸ Bottom: Regularly check all inflatable tubes

Pay careful attention to your control lines, leader lines and any stacking lines if flying a stack. Worn leader lines, sleeving or connection loops must be replaced immediately. Snapping a line at 20mph in your buggy or 5 metres off the water on your board is no joke.

Always wind your lines neatly and avoid dragging them across the ground. Walk towards them when winding in. Check the lines for any nicks or signs of wear. The lines start their life very smooth and slippery but may rough up with extensive use, specially if used a lot on sand. The sand grains can get in between the fibres and cause friction and wearing, interfering with flying and damaging the lines. Lines which have been used near water and sand, or are simply very dirty, can be rinsed, on their winder, under a running tap of cold water, teasing the lines with your fingers to help wash them clean. Hang the lines somewhere to dry, preferably out of direct sunlight, before packing away.

A well-looked-after set of flying lines should last you two or three years, if not longer, although this will reduce when you start adding the extra stress and loadings of buggying or kiteboarding. A set of kiteboarding lines, for instance, should be replaced every year or so.

Harnesses and harness loops are especially vulnerable to wear and tear with the heavy loading they carry. If you're using a harness check it over regularly for signs of wear, especially round the fastenings and the hook. Unexpected harness failure could

cause a real problem and crash helmets, especially any that have actually taken a few direct knocks, should also be regularly replaced as they become ineffective once damaged.

Buggies are made from stainless steel making them virtually maintenance free. Nevertheless, if your buggy is muddy or has been in salt water conditions you are well advised to hose it down thoroughly.

Inspect the frame for damage or cracks periodically. Don't attempt any repairs yourself; consult your dealer or Flexifoil International. You can clean the seat by hand washing it in warm soapy water, drying it out thoroughly before packing it away.

The wheel bearings will wear with use. This is unavoidable. They are made of hi-tensile rather than stainless steel. There are ways of prolonging their life with regular maintenance. Here's what to do:

- remove the wheel bolts occasionally and clean them.
- wash the wheels down with cold water and dry them, then spray with a Teflon type lubricant (bike chain type).
- check the plastic hub for damage or cracks and replace if necessary.
- the bearings themselves should be replaced when worn which is when they are reluctant to spin freely even when lubricated or have sideways movement.
- the same goes for the front fork bushes which are made from tough nylon. You should remove them and clean the assembly occasionally, replacing any worn bushes.

▸ *Check all moving parts on your buggy*

Kiteboards, especially those made from sandwich or other foam construction, are particularly vulnerable to the ravages of salt water and must be checked regularly for any knocks, bumps or cracking. Salt water in your board means the board is potentially fatally weakened. Check over your fins and their housings, likewise your bindings and their mountings and around the leash bung wherever that is. Don't take chances: take the board to your local dealer if you have the slightest doubt. They may have a repair workshop on site or will know where to send you or the board.

Adjusting your Dyneema lines

Dyneema flying lines have very little stretch but they do have some and the stretch is not necessarily even. You can generally fly all the stretch out of your lines in a couple of good sessions at the end of which you may find that one line has stretched more than another. This will cause your kite or wing to fly unevenly and needs to be remedied. Flexifoil line sets now come 'super-stretched' to avoid this kind of thing happening.

Dyneema flying lines have a length of sleeve roughly 30cm long at each end to help prevent them breaking with friction where knots are tied. The loop which you use to attach your flying lines to the kite or wing is made in this sleeved section. To make the

adjustment you need to do the following:

① Peg the loops at the free end of your lines to the ground using your ground stake. Unwind the lines fully and detach the handles or control bar.

② Pull on all or both lines together to identify which is the longer and by how much. Take the longer line and undo all the knots which form the loop at the unpegged end until the sleeve is free to move along the line. If you've been flying the kite in very strong wind these knots may have pulled very tight so be prepared with your best finger nails, teeth, etc.

③ Slide the sleeve along the flying line until it matches the other(s). If you can pull gently on all the lines as you do this it will help make it more accurate. If the sleeve is difficult to move try holding the end of Dyneema that's poking out and pulling the sleeve from the other end.

④ Retie the loop using a single thumb knot at the sleeve end towards the middle of the line to stop it slipping and then another thumb knot with the sleeved line doubled back on itself to form a good non-slip loop about 10cm wide or long. A thumb knot is the most basic form of knot. To tie one make a small loop where you want the knot and hold it between finger and thumb; pass the end of the line round the other side, back through the loop and pull tight and seal the ends with a lighter.

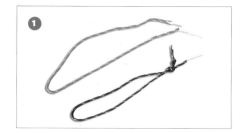

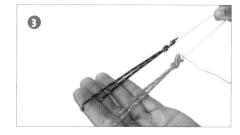

▸ *Adjusting your Dyneema lines*
▸ *Far right: Checking bridle lines*

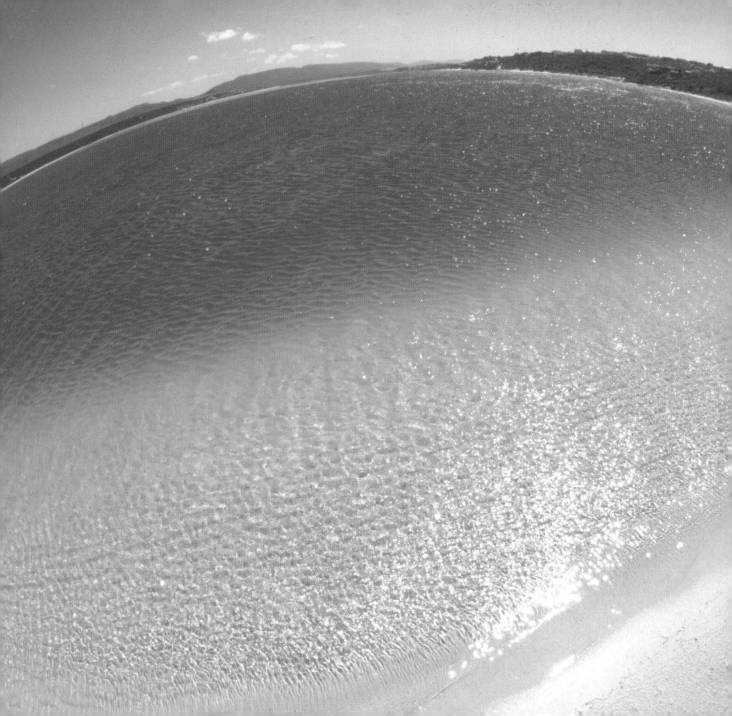

Where to go

THERE ARE LITERALLY thousands of good power kiting spots to visit on the thousands of miles of British coastline both on and off the beaten track. For pure recreational flying almost any good open site that conforms to all the safety guidelines explained at the beginning of the book will do. For the more serious stuff obviously other criteria, notably the one of having maximum space, and specifically kiteboarding where there is the pre-requirement for water too, will apply.

Once you start getting into buggying or boarding you would be much better off heading for one of the recognised sites where you might well find other drivers around, after all kiting is a social thing. Not only that, your sport may be covered by insurance or have support boats. If you really want to get out on your own on safari, why not join one of the members of the UK's Power Kite Sports Federation, which has a comprehensive list of approved sites for kite buggying or boarding for you to choose from and a season of organised events? You can either tag along or go to one of the other sites when they're all at an event somewhere else.

If anything there's a bit more freedom with kiteboarding. Buggies really need that hard, flat sand to run well; kiteboarders can launch from almost any type of beach. Saying that, restrictions do apply and once again you should consider joining the PKSF who's kiteboarding section, called the BKSA

(British Kite Surf Association), has an excellent website you can consult that lists literally hundreds of sites all around the UK with guidance as to where kiteboarding is and isn't practical or encouraged, schools, safety advice and so on.

Wherever you're thinking of going always check if local restrictions apply. In some cases you need only drive another five minutes to find restriction and hassle free facilities, as seems to be the case in West (restricted) and East (no restrictions) Wittering on the Sussex coast. In many places there are seasonal restrictions linked to holiday periods when the beaches and water are simply too busy to use. Contact details for the BKSA and IKO (International Kiteboarding Organisation) are in the following section. The IKO is an organisation that instructs and co-ordinates the instruction of kiteboard instructors for inflatable wings worldwide. As such it is a great resource of information regarding where to find kiteboarding schools around the world. (Contact details for the PKSF, BKSA and IKO are all in the Clubs and Associations later in this chapter).

Many dealers and retailers offer individual after-sales classes or formally structured courses which you're strongly advised to take up. And wherever you find a dealer you'll find their customers somewhere nearby who will already know the best places to go and how to do it. Why not think about a weekend or week long course at one of the power kite centres in the UK? An intensive course is the best way to learn and it's great fun to go away for the weekend with a

group of like-minded people for some intensive amusement and hands-on extreme sport action.

There are dozens of kiteboarding schools to choose from now, many linked to windsurf and other water and extreme sport centres, equipped with rescue craft etc. You'll now find kites and wings in many surf shops with boards and other kiteboarding equipment in many kite shops, many of which, as mentioned, offer tuition. Big organisations such as Club Med. and countless smaller companies are offering kiteboarding course holidays in various locations around the world.

It's a bit different for buggying. There are fewer recognised centres and schools but probably more informal tuition available. Saying that, there are a few dedicated full-time power kite centres in the UK where you can learn a range of power kiting activities, everything from flying your first Flexifoil to getting up on a kite board.

If the UK is well blessed with power kiting sites, so too are many other places around the world. Anywhere with good, big, empty beaches, shallow lagoon water and regular good strength winds. Lots of exotic warm water island locations that are big for windsurfing are already well established on the kiteboard circuit so you could do worse than start with a trip to Hawaii or Maui, the very nerve centre of all things surf. Closer to home, the Canary Islands offer great winter warmth and excellent wind and beaches, and France is the biggest European market for wind and water sports. But if you really want to go exotic then why not try New Caledonia in the south Pacific, the Madeleine Islands in

Canada, Dominican Republic, Martinique or Guadeloupe in the Caribbean, the Greek island of Paros, Tarifa in Spain, Australia, New Zealand, Hood River or The Gorge in America, Copacabana or Rio de Janeiro, Madagascar, Egypt, South Africa? Many locations now have fully equipped kiteboard schools or a well-established primary location plus good information regarding where else you can explore in the vicinity.

Clubs, societies and associations

At the time this book went to print, the UK power kiting scene had developed a plan and structure to try and bring together all the various power kiting disciplines under one umbrella organisation. This is no mean feat considering the wide range of applications and associations there are now in power kiting, from land boards and buggies to kiteboarding and snowkite. For serious and recreational traction action freaks in the UK that means there will now be somebody looking after your interests at both a practical level (teaching, event organisation, site data base etc.) and as regards future development, recognition and funding to develop the relative sports nationally and regionally. The organisation is called the Power Kite Sports Federation. The PKSF. will, eventually, combine some of the functions of all the various power kite sports' bodies in the UK, giving them one voice and more clout. A bit like building a big stack out of a number of individual kites. They plan offer

combined insurance policies for all types of power kiting activities, organise and sanction events, co-ordinate and certificate teaching and provide an important information resource for ALL power kite people post recognition of power kiting sports. In fact this will give recreational flyers a voice for the first time where previously only the more extreme activities were represented.

Contact for the PKSF should still be made via the existing individual bodies (who's contact details follow) which make up the new group. That will continue to be the case until new, permanent contact details are available, which they were not yet at print time (summer 2003) other than a provisional email address pending a more permanent organisation, also listed below.

Useful contacts

Power Kite Sports Federation (PKSF)
xkiteman@aol.com

British Kite Surf Association (BKSA)
www.kitesurfing.org
The BKSA has no permanent office or address in an effort to keep admin and other costs to a minimum. All its functions (membership, information, and so on) are run through its excellent website which is the primary means of contact. They also have a stand at all BKSA. events.

▶ The Flexifoil stand

International Kiteboarding Organisation (IKO)
www.ikorg.com
This is the place to hit if you want information about the international scene, particularly the whereabouts of approved kiteboarding schools everywhere in the world including Britain.

British Buggy Club (BBC)
Email: info@buggy.demon.co.uk
www.buggy.demon.co.uk
PO Box 4015
Smethwick
Warley
West Midlands B67 6HJ
UK

Para Kart Association (PKA)
www.pka.org.uk

Kite Landboard Association (KLA)
www.kla.org
 Scottish Power Kite Association (SPKA)
www.spka.co.uk

Irish Power Kite Association (IPKA)
No contact available

UK Snowkite Club
No contact available yet at print time.

Magazines, publications, videos and DVDs

There are four English language full colour kiteboarding and power kite magazines available in the UK, and others abroad. *Kitesurf 1* is an English language title from French publisher Custom Publishing (the French have strong claims to have invented kiteboarding) and *Kitesurf* magazine comes from UK publisher Arcwind. *Kiteworld* is a more recent starter from XCMedia and *Powerkite* magazine was launched in 2003. All are widely available through specialist shops and increasingly through the newsagents' network.

 All cover kiteboarding events, tips, advice, board, wing and other equipment tests and pages and pages of colour photos from all round the world that will have you really drooling – blue lagoons, tropical sun and deserted palm-fringed white sand beaches. Just the thing to keep your spirits up on those grim, grey, 7mm wetsuit northern hemisphere winter days. *Kitesurf 1* also carries regular landboard, buggy and snowkite features. *Kiteworld* also covers the rapidly expanding snowkite scene. *Kiteboarder* magazine is published in America with similar content to the two European magazines. Many other countries now have their own dedicated kiteboard title or, like Australia, have regular kiteboard supplements available in the established surf or windsurf mags. As you can imagine, the internet is awash with kiteboard stuff, just type kiteboard, kitesurf or flysurf into your

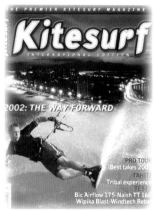

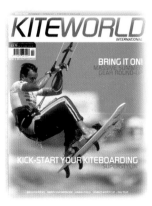

search engine and see where you get!

There's also one specialist landboard and mountainboard magazine available in the UK. It's called *ATB* (All Terrain Boarding) mag and covers all aspects of ATB-ing: downhill, flat and kite powered. This is definitely one to ask for in the specialist shops at present but worth having as it's the only UK specialist mag covering the subject. If you have difficulty finding it why not take out a subscription for 12 issues per year, contact: ATBmag, Ham Cottage, Ham, Axminster, Devon EX13 7HL; info@atbmag.com

As for DVD and video, kiteboarding being such a very visual thing, there are now countless DVDs and videos available crammed full of great action shots, some from competition, others trips, others simply for the hell of it (almost all with the obligatory ha-ha-ha 'wipeouts' section). And there are quite a few teaching videos too. All in all there are far too many to list here but a quick visit to your local kite or surf dealer is sure to be rewarded with a good selection to choose from. Flexifoil themselves currently have two pure entertainment power kite video titles available: 'Power Trip', a 20 minute showcase of all sorts of power kiting nonsense with the Flexifoil crew all going ape crazy bonkers in Senegal, and 'Airheads', a 45 minute blast from Maui featuring not just the Flexi boys but a large number of the world's other top riders who are based there and some superb kiteboarding action.

One excellent instruction video well worth checking out is a made-in-the-USA, or rather Hawaii, package called 'The Boost'. It's a double cassette teaching video, with tape one dedicated to all the basic starting up stuff and tape two going on to look at more complex manoeuvres and tricks. In fact there are various manufacturers' videos out there as well and at least one instruction video would be a sound investment and sensible back-up to have for when school is out and it's time to get out on your own.

Dealer details

If you're reading this and expecting to find a long list of names, addresses and telephone numbers for your nearest stockist then look no further. Because there isn't one. It wouldn't be possible to print them all and it wouldn't be fair to leave any out.

Even in the UK the number of Flexifoil stockists is enormous and, while some of them might not carry all the really serious buggy and boarding equipment, it would be unfair just to list the main dealers. Every one of them, even the little ones, have helped to make Flexifoil what it is today, one of the biggest names in worldwide power kiting circles.

There are obvious places to look for Flexifoil products, kite, surf and windsurf shops being the places to start. But you'll also find racks of Flexifoil kites and other accessories in many enlightened extreme sports, outdoor pursuits, rollerblade and juggling shops. The easiest way to find the nearest appropriate store for you is to contact Flexifoil International direct who will be happy to put you in touch. To save you the embarrassment of a polite 'no' on the phone, Flexifoil do not sell direct to the public at fantastically reduced factory prices; you must use their established dealer network.

Flexifoil International
27 Regal Drive
Soham
Ely
Cambridgeshire CB7 5BE
Tel: 01353 723131
Fax: 01353 722311
Email: info@flexifoil.co.uk
www.flexifoil.com

As much as they are in demand in the UK, Flexifoil kites and traction equipment are well known and similarly available in countries all over the world including: United States, Canada, South Africa, Australia, New Zealand, Germany, France, Spain, Holland, Italy, Belgium, Norway, Sweden, Finland, Austria, Denmark Switzerland, Republic of Ireland, Mexico, Brazil, Chile, Cyprus, Bahrain. Again, for full information, contact Flexifoil direct or visit www.flexifoil.com

Available line lengths and strengths

Size of kite		Recreational use (wind up to 15mph)	Heavy use (windover 15mph)
2-3m	Main lines	300lb	500lb
	Brake lines	200lb	200lb
4m	Main lines	500lb	500lb
	Brake lines	200lb	300lb
up to 5m	Brake lines	500lb	500lb
	Main lines	300lb	300lb
5m +	Brake lines	500lb	500lb
	Main lines	300lb	300lb

Index